VANGUARD SERIES

EDITOR: MARTIN WINDRO

THE
SHERMAN TANK
in British Service
1942-45

Text by the late

JOHN SANDARS

Colour plates by

MICHAEL ROFFE and MIKE CHAPPELL

OSPREY PUBLISHING LONDON

Published in 1980 by
Osprey Publishing Ltd
Member company of the George Philip Group
12–14 Long Acre, London WC2E 9LP
© Copyright 1980 Osprey Publishing Ltd

ISBN 0 85045 361 5

Filmset in Great Britain
Printed in Hong Kong

The author wishes to thank the Imperial War
Museum and the Kent and Sharpshooters Yeomanry
for permission to use photographs from their
collections, and the Curator and staff of the RAC
Tank Museum for assistance with his researches;
also the following (all now retired from the Army)
who were kind enough to discuss their experiences of
the Sherman tank with him: Col. P. H. Hordern,
D.S.O., O.B.E. (RTR); Lt.-Col. K. J. Hill (RTR);
Lt.-Col. J. Blackater, D.S.O., T.D. (Gordons; 116
RAC); Maj. K. Macksey, M.C. (RTR); Maj. D.
Covill, M.B.E., D.C.M. (10 H); Maj. W. H. Sale,
M.B.E., M.C. (3 CLY); Maj. D. F. Underhill (Staffs
Yeo); MQMS J. Coward, M.M. (10 H); Sgt. P.
Robinson, M.M. (GG); Corporal A. Hodgkinson
(51 RTR); Corporal J. Taylor (Notts SF Yeo);
Trooper A. Eldridge (10 H); and Sgt. R. L. Cessford
(1 Derby Yeo), who also kindly allowed the use of
his sketches made in Italy.
    Numerous written works were consulted in the
preparation of this book, including the various
publications on the Sherman by Chamberlain &
Ellis; *British & Commonwealth Armoured Formations* by
Duncan Crow; *British Tank Markings and Names* by
B. T. White; *Sherman* by R. P. Hunnicut; and
various campaign, formation and unit histories.

Development

As the Second World War progressed it became clear that Great Britain, with her limited design and production capacity, could not keep pace with the tank losses already suffered in France, and currently being experienced both in the desert and at sea on the way there, while at the same time equipping the new armoured formations that were being trained at home. Help had to be sought from the Americans, who not only had the industrial capacity to provide the necessary machines, but also the flexibility and speed of response to do so in an acceptably short time.

Three main types of American tank were supplied, initially under the 'cash and carry' scheme, and later 'Lend-Lease'. The first, the M3 Stuart, was a light tank more suited for reconnaissance than the main battlefield, but which nevertheless made a welcome addition to tank strength in the Middle East in late 1941; then in mid-1942 came the M3 Medium Lee/Grant (see Vanguard 6, *The Lee/Grant Tanks in British Service*), which was essentially a stop-gap until a properly designed tank, with the 75mm gun that was needed to meet the Germans on equal terms, could be produced. This was the M4 Sherman, which finally reached Egypt in time for the battle of Alamein in October 1942. It was a general-purpose medium which not only became the basic American tank for the rest of the war, but was also the type most widely used by the British Army, not to mention Indian and Commonwealth formations, from then on.

The M4 was conceived in 1940 while the in-terim M3 was also still in the design stage. The American emphasis was on ease and speed of production rather than sophistication and innovation in the finished product, so the mechanical parts were initially identical to those of the M3, which the Sherman was destined to replace on the production lines of the 11 major plants (including two factory complexes specifically built for tank production) given over to making it. The radial, air-cooled, aircraft-type petrol engine, with its drive to sprockets at the front of the vehicle through a controlled differential transmission, was thus the same as that in the M3 (and resulted in almost as tall a tank, since the prop shaft had to pass from the centre of the engine under the turret basket). Also the simple but robust bogies with vertical volute springs and rubber block tracks were also well tried from earlier American designs. The important innovations were a new cast hull, and a large cast turret with all-round traverse housing a 75mm gun and, in British fashion, the radio set.

Development changes were being made even before the first vehicles went into action in the autumn of 1942. The short M2 75mm gun with which the prototypes were equipped was replaced with the longer M3; and since it became clear that the casting of the huge one-piece hulls would form a bottle-neck, a fabricated welded hull was also put into production early on and eventually became the standard type. The first 300 supplied to the British were mostly cast-hull M4A1 Sherman

A diesel-engined Sherman III marked as belonging to an armoured regimental HQ, with its 'sunshade' camouflage rigged to make it look like a lorry. This disguise was used extensively before Alamein, and was the real reason that tanks had side rails fitted. Although the Shermans came with 'Ameri'cans, fuel was still supplied in four-gallon 'flimsies', as seen here, at this time.

IIs, but there were also some welded-hull M4 Sherman Is and IIIs among them; some had been withdrawn, on Roosevelt's orders, from American units to make up this number. From then on development was continuous; at a very early stage

The inside of the turret was fairly cramped. Here a crew member (Canadian judging from the cap badge) sleeps under the gun between the gunner's seat and the commander's folding one. Some of the lavish supply of spare periscope heads can be seen round the gunner's seat.

the M3 type bogies with the return roller on top were replaced by new ones with rollers mounted at the rear, and solid as well as spoked road wheels began to appear in some cases. Then, as aircraft engine production was not unnaturally required for aeroplanes, alternative power plants were introduced. First came the M4A2 Sherman III with twin General Motors diesel engines; then the M4A3 Sherman IV with a specially designed light alloy Ford V8 petrol engine. The M4A4 Sherman V had a composite unit of vast size and weight (the hull had to be lengthened to take it) made up of five Chrysler car engines geared to a common drive; 'Heath Robinson', but just the sort of thing the American car industry could turn out without costly and time-consuming design and retooling. Finally, a few Caterpillar diesels were used for the M4A6 Sherman VII, but it is not clear if any of these in fact came to the British. (The M4A5 Mark VI designation was not a Sherman but was used for the rather similar Canadian Ram tank.) Most British Shermans were Marks III, V, I and II in that order.

At the same time hulls, suspensions and armament were continually developed. Three-piece bolted nose transmission covers gave way to single-piece cast ones; vision slits were eliminated; a wider gun mantlet, the M34A1, replaced the narrow M34; appliqué armour was welded over vulnerable areas alongside ammunition lockers and petrol tanks as well as round the turret fronts, and two different types of metal track were introduced to replace the rubber types. In some cases these modifications were built into new vehicles, but in others old ones were reworked, so it was possible to see all the various permutations right up to the end of the war.

More radical developments involved the fitting of a larger turret and 76mm gun to the Sherman IVs in early 1944, and retrospectively to other Marks, with a steeper 47° front hull plate, and wet-protected stowages for ammunition. Another variant had a rolled/cast front on the welded hull; and some were fitted with a 105mm howitzer. Finally a new suspension system using wider, centre-toothed tracks and horizontal volute sprung bogies (HVSS) appeared in late 1944.

Although the British received some of the 76mm gun tanks, denoting them by the suffix A (i.e.

Sherman IIA), they produced their own improved anti-tank version by fitting a 17pdr. gun in a modified original M4 turret, using the suffix C for vehicles (mostly Mark Vs) so converted, and nicknaming them 'Fireflies'. They also used some of the 105mm versions (suffix B) in Italy; but did not receive the up-armoured M4A3E2 'Jumbos' which the Americans employed as assault tanks in North-West Europe, since they already had the British-made Churchill for that rôle. Various local operational modifications were also made by the British to standard tanks, including the fitting of the American-designed Culin device for breaking through hedgerows in Normandy; and rocket rails on the turrets of tanks of the Coldstream Guards, towards the end of the war. British Shermans fitted with the wide 23in. track and HVSS had the further suffix Y added to their mark numbers, and the few with cast glacis plates were known as 'hybrids'.

As well as the gun tanks, which are the main subject of this book, many Shermans were extensively converted to form the 'Funnies'—the specialized armour used in the Normandy landings and elsewhere. These included DD (swimming) tanks, Flails and other mine-clearing devices, bridging tanks, Kangaroos (personnel carriers) and even gun-towers (17pdrs. in Italy), while in armoured regiments and artillery units specially equipped versions were used as OPs and Command/Rear Link tanks. In various REME units, not all with armoured troops, turretless Sherman armoured recovery vehicles (ARVs) were part of the establishment.

Although at no time, even when first introduced at Alamein, was the Sherman superior on a gun/armour basis to the best current enemy tanks, its reliability, potential for up-gunning and other development, and above all the sheer numbers available (in North-West Europe it was estimated that the British could afford to lose six tanks for every enemy one destroyed) enabled it to fill a vital gap in the British armoury from 1943 on. Despite individual tank-vs.-tank inferiority in some respects, this enabled the British Army to achieve overall armoured superiority in the long run.

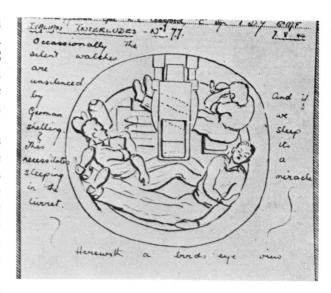

One of a series of sketches of life in Shermans, sent home from Italy by Mr R. L. Cessford, then a corporal in 'C' Sqn., 1st Derbyshire Yeomanry—the recce regiment of 6th Armoured Division. Crews normally slept on the ground beside their tanks, but, as shown here, they could at a pinch squeeze into the tank itself and more or less stretch out. (Cessford)

A Grant and a Sherman III at range practice in Egypt. The Sherman was almost as bulky as the Grant, being in fact only four inches lower, but with its main gun in the turret was able to fire from hull-down positions—always supposing it could find any for a large tank in terrain such as this.

North Africa

The first Shermans to see action with the British Army arrived in Egypt during August–September 1942; but they were not ready for battle, following British and desert modifications, repainting to local colour schemes, and crew training, until late October at Alamein. When the battle started there were 252 Shermans in the field, in a dozen regiments. Priority was given to equipping all the heavy squadrons in the regiments of one brigade in each of X Corps' two armoured divisions. The remainder went to equip one squadron in each regiment of the second brigade in 10th Armoured Division, and 9th Brigade, which was temporarily an integral part of the New Zealand division in XXX Corps. The second heavy squadrons in the regiments of these formations were equipped with Grants. 7th Armoured Division (see Vanguard 1, *British 7th Armoured Division*) in XIII Corps received no Shermans. (Armoured regiments in the desert at that time consisted of two 16-tank heavy squadrons and one light squadron of Crusaders, in some cases augmented by Stuarts.)

The Axis defences at Alamein consisted of a continuous belt of interconnected minefields, dotted with outposts, stretching from the sea to the impassable Quattara Depression 35 miles inland. Behind this came the main defence line of Italian infantry positions interspersed with German units. The whole was in places several miles deep, and was supported by dug-in artillery and mixed battlegroups of German and Italian armour in rear, while the few mobile reserves were further west in the open desert. Montgomery's plan to crack this nut explains the distribution of the avail-

Working on the Wright Whirlwind engine of a Sherman I. The plugs, etc., for the lower cylinders of this radial unit were inaccessible without lifting the engine. The tops of the two vertical fuel tanks, for high-octane aircraft petrol, can be seen on either side in front of the engine. (Sharpshooters)

able Shermans, which were his most powerful tanks. XIII Corps was to feint against the southern end of the line and was then to be available as a reserve, while XXX Corps, which was mainly infantry with armoured support units, advanced by night through the minefields and engaged the main defences in the northern sector. They were to be followed by the armour of X Corps, moving through rapidly cleared lanes in the minefields; the tanks would then debouch behind the main defence line and hold off armoured counter-attacks while the infantry 'crumbled' up the static positions free from armoured interference. A break-out was then finally to be made, probably by the New Zealand division with its incorporated armoured brigade, and X Corps would advance westwards in pursuit of the beaten enemy.

In the event delays meant that the armour was not clear of the minefields by daylight, and in consequence the Sherman's debut was a bloody one fought out amongst mines, in open desert with

There were official Middle East camouflage schemes and patterns for Shermans which at least some units used. Here, at the end of the North African campaign, Sherman Is of 3rd CLY wear that laid down in June 1943 of Blue-Black over Light Mud; from December 1942 it had been Dark Green over Desert Pink, and before that a contrasting colour, at the CO's discretion, over Light or Portland Stone. (Sharpshooters)

Sherman IIs of 'C' Sqn., 9th Lancers shortly after issue. The track-guards and side rails, as well as the round-topped turret bin, were standard desert modifications. Markings visible on the original are squadron sign on turret sides, troop numbers on bins, 1st Armoured Division sign on left track-guard, and unit sign—white 86 on red square—on right track-guards; untypically, aerial pennants are not being flown, a possible sign that these tanks were in training when the photograph was taken.

little cover, against dug-in anti-tank guns and hull-down tanks, of which at least the few 88mms and the 'Mark IV Specials' (PzKpfw IVFs) out-classed it. The poet Keith Douglas was glad of his fast, low-silhouette Crusader as he watched the bulky Shermans trying to find cover; but another officer, at that time also still in a Crusader squad-ron, was envious of their ability to pick off tanks at ranges that clearly surprised the enemy, while he impotently watched no less than six rounds from his 2pdr. bounce off a German PzKpfw III at

500 yards range. Others experienced a direct hit on the Sherman turret from a 105mm field gun, causing no more than a red glow inside, and up to five hits from the 50mm anti-tank gun which failed to penetrate.

For the next week the dogfight continued while the British armour struggled unsuccessfully to break out into open desert. Losses mounted until a stalemate threatened, but they succeeded in holding off numerous counter-attacks neverthe-less, and destroyed many enemy tanks and guns that Rommel was less able to afford than they were. At the start of November Montgomery withdrew the bulk of X Corps, refitted it, and side-stepped it further north to exploit successes by the Australians near the coast. Here the New Zealanders, led by the 9th Armoured Brigade—who suffered 75 per cent losses when they were caught on the enemy gun line as dawn broke on 2 November—at last forced a gap through which X Corps were able to move and engage the enemy armour and anti-tank guns directly in open desert at Tel-el-Aqaqqir. Here they fought the Afrika Korps to a standstill until the main de-fences, denuded of support, collapsed further south; and Rommel started the long retreat to Tunisia on 4 November.

The pursuit got away to a slow start due to traffic problems, lack of fuel, and torrential rain (this was the only occasion that one trooper ever remembers using the driver's hood provided with the Sherman). It soon became clear that X Corps had suffered too severely to fully accomplish its pursuit rôle, so the less heavily engaged 7th Armoured Division, with its geriatric Grants, had to make much of the running. As 8th Army moved west the problems were further complicated by the need to immobilize formations and use their trucks to maintain a decreasing armoured spearhead until the ports of Tobruk and Benghazi could be put

back into full operation. There were, however, some Sherman-equipped units up with the hunt most of the time, and it was here that their steady reliability, especially that of the diesel-engined Mark IIIs, began to show up favourably compared with other types.

The general mode of pursuit was by regimental groups, each with their recce troop (scout cars) and light squadrons out ahead, and one heavy squadron on either side of a central column of HQ and supply vehicles, a field gun battery, AA and AT troops, and a motor infantry company. With their ability to fire HE semi-indirect the Shermans were increasingly able to deal with rearguard ambushes, once these had revealed themselves, without having to call in the guns and infantry. H. W. Schmidt, Rommel's erstwhile ADC, who was commanding rearguard detachments of 90 Light Division, describes the rapid elimination of an 88mm gun by two Shermans that it could not even see, as well as the inability of his 50mm Paks, the main German anti-tank guns

Sherman II, possibly of 'C' Sqn., The Queen's Bays, entering Mersa Matruh. In action tanks quickly assumed this worn, dusty look, which contrasts markedly with the newly issued vehicles in earlier photographs. The stowage of bedrolls and packs is typical for the desert, but not for later campaigns.

at that time, to penetrate the Sherman turrets, although they could pierce the side armour at battle ranges.

As the advance continued more 8th Army units had their Grants replaced by Shermans, and by March 1943 even 7th Armoured Division had them. At about the same time 6th Armoured Division in 1st Army, which had landed in Tunisia in November, also received its first Shermans to replace the mixture of Valentines and Crusaders in its 26th Armoured Brigade. Here the whole units were given Shermans, since there were no light squadrons; and as they also used the European organization of 61 tanks to a regiment instead of the 52 normal in the Middle East, they ended up more powerful than their 8th Army counterparts.

On the 8th Army front the battle of Medenine in early March was won virtually without the use of British armour. At Mareth, X Corps was initially held in reserve while XXX Corps attacked the old French defensive line frontally with infantry, and the New Zealanders, with 8th Armoured Brigade, made a left hook around its inland end. When it became clear that the frontal attack was failing Montgomery sent 1st Armoured Division from X Corps to join the New Zealand thrust, which was also delayed at the Tebaga gap. Here an operation not unlike the break-out from

Alamein was organized; in fact it was even given the same codename, 'Supercharge'. Under cover of the heaviest close-support aerial bombardment of the campaign so far, the New Zealanders, led by the Sherman squadrons of 8th Armoured Brigade, broke through the enemy positions, which included elements of 21st Panzer Division. This success opened the gap for 1st Armoured Division to pass through and form up in open country for a night advance towards el Hamma behind the Mareth Line. Drivers and co-drivers remember the difficulty, even from the comparatively high driver's position of the Sherman, of following the tank ahead in the dust and dark; although the blue flames shooting from the exhausts made this easier for them than it was for drivers of wheeled transport, it was tiring work. In this case, the attack did not start until the moon was up, and, being a novelty, caught the enemy unprepared. The advance was made with two regiments abreast in the lead and the third shepherding the immediate support vehicles along behind; but unfortunately frequent wadis and

9

Tanks of 'A' Sqn., 3rd CLY *en route* to Sicily in the hold of a Landing Ship Tank (LST). The crew of the nearest tank, 'Ailsa', seem to have a mixture of the infantry-type rimmed helmets and the newer rimless RAC pattern. Side coamings and old ammunition boxes have been welded to this tank to provide improved storage. (Sharpshooters)

result that probably could not have been achieved by any type of Allied tank at that time except the Sherman, since the Churchill, although more heavily armoured, only carried a 6pdr. gun incapable of effectively engaging anti-tank guns. (See Vanguard 13, *The Churchill Tank.*) Unfortunately, it did not prove possible to exploit the result of this gallant action.

As 8th Army advanced northwards towards Tunis, driving the Axis out of the Akarit position mainly by infantry and artillery action, and 1st Army kept up the pressure from the west, General Alexander was able to co-ordinate the two armies and switch formations between them as required. Thus both 1st and 7th Armoured Divisions, among others, went over to 1st Army before the final assault on Tunis, while the rest of 8th Army contained the enemy around Enfidaville. Some units managed to repaint their tanks green for the switch, but others got no paint, and one even ended up painting them black! The final attack to capture Tunis itself was made from the west on a two-division front, by two infantry divisions followed by 6th and 7th Armoured Divisions abreast, all with heavy air and artillery support. After the initial breakthrough by infantry aided by Churchills, the armour was unleashed and advanced in textbook fashion through enemy units, some of which still fought fiercely, while others were beginning to disintegrate. With the advent of the Tiger tank, 75mm anti-tank gun, and hollow-charge AP ammunition for some low-velocity German guns, not to mention an increased proportion of PzKpfw IVF tanks with the long 75mm gun, the Shermans were qualitatively at more of a disadvantage in Tunisia than in the desert, but their increased numbers, HE-firing gun, and reliability enabled them to compete satisfactorily.

All resistance did not end in Tunis, and a certain amount of fierce mopping up was still to be done. It was perhaps prophetic of their rôle in future campaigns that one of the last actions by Shermans in North Africa was carried out by the Lothians on a beach; not in this instance making a landing, but forcing a way through the coastal town of Hamman Lif.

other obstacles slowed it just sufficiently for the enemy to form an *ad hoc* anti-tank screen, which halted it at dawn near el Hamma. This held up the advance until the remnants of 21st Panzer had sorted themselves out and 15th Panzer had moved up in support, so it was not possible to break through to the coast and cut off the troops in the Mareth Line; nevertheless this threat to their rear forced the Germans to abandon it and retire.

Much of the fighting in Tunisia involved either holding or breaking through the various passes in the mountain ranges. In April 1st Army forced that at Fondouk in an effort to cut off the Axis troops retiring before 8th Army in the Kairouan area. Here, due to the failure of untried American troops to capture the flanking hills, 26th Armoured Brigade had to make a frontal attack down the pass practically on its own, through minefields and in the face of defiladed anti-tank guns. The attack was led by 17th/21st Lancers in a manner reminiscent of Balaclava, and despite the loss of nearly 40 tanks the pass was taken and three enemy tanks and 33 guns were destroyed—a

Sicily and Italy

Waterproofed Sherman landing from an LCT at Reggio. Fabric sealing round the main and hull guns, and the rectangular exhaust trunk, are all part of the waterproofing to allow tanks to wade ashore, here clearly not needed in the event. The unit sign, 173 on a blue-over-brown square, was the standard Middle East sign for the senior regiment in an Army tank brigade at that time, so this tank is presumably part of a Churchill-equipped unit. Four-inch smoke dischargers can be seen on the turret side.

It was here, from mid-1943 until the end of the war, that the Sherman really came into its own, demonstrating its ability to perform almost any armoured rôle in the absence of the more specialized tanks used in North-West Europe. Although the German Tigers and Panthers were both much superior in armour and hitting power, the backbone of the armoured forces on both sides was the larger number of reliable general-purpose tanks; the Allied Sherman and the ageing German PzKpfw IV.

As there were no British Cruiser tanks in Italy, and the Churchill infantry support tanks were almost all of the earlier Marks with the 6pdr. gun, not only was the Sherman used to equip the armoured divisions and brigades (which included Canadian, Polish, New Zealand and South African as well as British formations); but armoured reconnaissance regiments had a mixture of Shermans and turretless Stuarts (two of each per troop) in place of the Cromwell Cruisers used by such units in North-West Europe, and Churchill regiments initially had up to half the troops in each squadron equipped with Shermans to augment their firepower and make up numbers. The terrain also necessitated certain specialized armour, so Shermans saw service as tankdozers and fascine carriers, while many units had the American Sherman M32 recovery vehicles (which, having heavy-duty jibs, were superior to the British Mark I variety). Attempts were also made locally to convert Shermans into bridgelayers, but the Valentine 'Scissors' and Churchill 'Ark' were mostly used in this rôle. Later on Sherman 'Funnies' similar to those in 79th Armoured Division, such as minesweeping 'Crabs', personnel-carrying 'Kangaroos', and swimming 'DDs', were also used in Italy.

The armoured regiments themselves dispensed with their light regiments of Crusaders before crossing the Mediterranean, and had all three squadrons and their HQs equipped with 75mm gun Shermans, while their reconnaissance troops had turretless Stuarts. In 1944 76mm gun Shermans were issued, initially one per troop but later in many cases completely replacing the

75mm gun versions in an effort to improve anti-tank capability. Some 105mm gun Shermans were also provided, two to each squadron HQ as close-support tanks, and eventually a few 17pdr. 'Fireflies' also, but never in the numbers seen in North-West Europe.

Two reduced-strength armoured brigades, the 4th and 23rd, landed with the British invasion force on the south-east corner of Sicily in mid-July 1943. The landings were largely unopposed, but the Shermans saw some stiff fighting later, giving close support to the infantry moving up the east coast and in the final stages in the north-east corner of the island. Naval gunfire support was much used, and on at least one occasion when the proximity of friendly troops to the target forced a naval OP to stop firing with a Cruiser, the leader of their protecting troop of Shermans took over the bombardment, with less weight but more accuracy, with his own 75mms. The use of tanks as artillery was to become typical of this theatre more than any other, as was their close working with infantry. Another sign of the changing times and close-country fighting was the loss of a regimental CO to snipers in the fighting around the Primasole bridge, while trying to cross the River Simento and break out into the Catania plain.

In September 1943, 23rd Armoured Brigade landed at Salerno on the mainland of Italy with the American 5th Army. Again, this was not an assault landing for the Shermans, but they had some stiff fighting before the bridgehead was secure. Subsequently 7th Armoured Division landed there and fought up the west coast through Naples to the River Garigliano with 5th Army, while 4th Armoured Brigade landed at Taranto and went up the east coast to the Sangro with the British 8th Army. As armoured divisions had, by this stage in the war, been reduced to only one armoured brigade each, the two formations had approximately equal numbers of tanks.

The actual fighting, which had gradually changed through Tunisia and Sicily, was a far cry from the pursuit after Alamein, but still at this stage gave occasional opportunities for the armour to take the lead and sweep forward in open formation. For the most part, however, units fought split up in close support of the infantry—in the 'I' tank rôle, in effect. The country was divided down the centre by mountains, while on either side poor roads, scattered compact villages, dense vineyards and frequent ridges, rivers and streams across the line of advance made it ideal for defence. Although the Luftwaffe was to be less of a nuisance than in Tunisia, mines of all sorts, snipers, mortars, and infantry anti-tank weapons of the bazooka type were all to prove serious problems to Shermans and their crews, as were the many self-propelled anti-tank guns, 88mm Flak and Pak, and German tanks, which now included a fair number of Tigers and Panthers. Nevertheless, the combination of rugged reliability and the 75mm gun enabled them to hold their own in a slow and frustrating northward advance, making full use of co-operation with the other arms. In some instances the Sherman's mobility clearly surprised the enemy, as when a squadron climbed

The Chrysler Multibank engine of a Sherman V. This is one of the later models, and all five carburettors can be seen at the top. The engine has been turned through 180° since lifting from the tank, and the radiators at the front of the engine can be seen beyond the fitter squatting on top.

out of a gully to attack the breech ends of the German guns at one stage of the Sangro battle.

By November, however, deteriorating weather slowed the advance even further, with tanks frequently becoming completely bogged. It finally came to a halt facing the first of the major defensive lines across the country, the Gustav Line, running from Ortona to the Garigliano through Cassino. By this time 7th Armoured Division and 4th Armoured Brigade were needed at home to prepare for the Normandy invasion, and left the theatre; but 6th Armoured Division arrived in time for the winter fighting around Cassino, together with Canadian, Polish and New Zealand armoured units equipped with Shermans. The attempt to turn the Gustav Line by a landing at Anzio was assisted by a single regiment from 23rd Armoured Brigade, which played a significant part in defeating several fierce counter-attacks on the bridgehead before this brigade was returned to Egypt and replaced in Italy by 7th Armoured Brigade. At the same time armoured strength was built up over the winter by the arrival of 9th Armoured Brigade (which had been part of the New Zealand Division at Alamein), the new South African Armoured Division, and the 21st and 25th Tank Brigades with their mixture of Shermans and Churchills.

When the Gustav Line finally collapsed in May 1944 following the murderous battles around Cassino, and an eventual breakthrough by the

On the move in Italy; a Sherman not only carrying infantry but also towing an artillery limber and a 17pdr. anti-tank gun.

French into the Liri Valley, the 25th Tank Brigade assaulted its northward extension, known as the Hitler Line. Here, among other horrors, the defences included dug-in Panther tank turrets. Despite severe losses the combination of the Churchill's armour and all-terrain mobility, and the Sherman's firepower, coupled with the determination of the Canadian infantry, told eventually, and by the end of May the way was clear for the advance to continue to the north. 8th Army was now concentrated on the centre and right of the line with 6th Armoured Division and 9th Armoured Brigade supporting 78th Infantry Division on their left flank, while 7th Armoured Brigade pushed on up the Adriatic coast. The American 5th Army was on the west coast and entered Rome on 4 June.

Once again the armour was split up, with regiments working with infantry brigades, or subdivided into even smaller groupings. The advance was an exhausting series of small ambush actions in close country, with numerous detours and delays where the poor roads had been demolished at crossings over the many streams and rivers, or had collapsed under the unaccustomed weight of traffic. It was often necessary to keep the tanks off what roads there were in order

A variant which saw much use in Italy; the Sherman tank-dozer. This particular vehicle (in fact photographed in North-West Europe) has the heavy net and hessian strip camouflage used by some units in preference to vegetation, while the gun is wrapped in what looks like sacking, presumably to prevent reflections.

to preserve them for wheeled transport. The opposition, partly composed of German para-troops, had the added advantage of observation from the hills. Resistance gradually stiffened until on 20 June the next defensive line was reached, running through Lake Trasimene, the scene of one of Hannibal's victories. Here, despite it being summer, operations were again hindered by torrential rain, and the Sherman units found the turretless Stuarts of their recce troops in-valuable in bringing up supplies and evacuating wounded in conditions where half-tracks, let alone wheeled vehicles, could not cope, and in many cases under fire. Some of the older Shermans which had had their turrets removed for use as fascine carriers were also used for these duties. The defences included tanks, guns and Nebel-werfers well dug-in and concealed in good defen-sive positions, and the Sherman's ability to fire AP, smoke and HE as required was fortunate. One regiment surprised not only the enemy, but also its own superiors, by assaulting a supposedly 'tank-proof' hill with marked success; but op-portunities for spectacular strokes such as this were rare.

By the end of the month the Germans were again in retreat, but their stubborn fighting in the Trasimene Line had blunted the Allied offensive and reduced the chances of their breaking out into

the north Italian plains before winter 1944–45. The advance continued against the usual skilful rearguards; many units, such as those in 6th Arm-oured Division, had been continuously in action for nearly three months by the time they reached Florence in early August, and neither men nor tanks were at their best—although the Shermans kept going well under the circumstances, not, as one writer put it, 'having been designed as moun-tain goats'. The situation then stabilized again in front of the mountainous Gothic Line based on the Apennines, the last major obstacle before the supposedly more open country of northern Italy and the Po Valley.

At this point a certain amount of Allied re-organization took place. It was decided to breach the line with the whole of 8th Army on the Adriatic coast. Infantry divisions, with the tank brigades attached, would break through while 6th Armoured Division kept up pressure on their left flank in the mountains. 1st Armoured Division, which had just arrived in Italy, was in reserve to exploit the breakthrough. It was also at this time that the armoured regiments began to receive 76mm Shermans, and during the subsequent autumn fighting, 105mms and the first 17pdr. Fireflies.

The Gothic Line itself was not heavily fortified, but made full use of ideal defensive country and good observation. After the complicated move across the Apennines to regroup 8th Army, the line was successfully breached at the start of September, and 1st Armoured Division tried to exploit while 6th Armoured Division advanced slowly on the left. Here they were often employed as artillery, using their Sherman 75s for such re-finements as bouncing delay-fused shells off the mountain ridges to airburst over the reverse slopes. The country behind the Gothic Line was still interspersed with numerous rivers and banks, but gave less cover than before, which prevented any real break-out and made 1st Armoured Division's progress painful and methodical rather than dashing. By the start of October rainy weather was further reducing tank mobility, and it tended to become an engineers' battle, with bulldozers, fascines, and Bailey bridges increas-ingly needed if the tanks were to get anywhere. Nevertheless progress was made until Ravenna

Mud on the Garigliano. A Sherman with metal cleat tracks, and desert-style cookers and pots slung from the back, waits in front of one (right) with solid bogie wheels, and the later wide M34A1 combination gun mount, but the original three-part bolted nosepiece.

was reached in December, when 8th Army was finally forced to stop for the winter, and several of the armoured regiments temporarily abandoned their Shermans in order to help out as foot-soldiers in the line.

By the time the final advances were made in the late spring of 1945 further developments and re-organizations had taken place. 25th Tank Brigade had been converted to an assault brigade on the lines of 79th Armoured Division, with flame-throwing Churchill 'Crocodile' and mine-sweeping Sherman 'Crab' tanks; and one regiment, 7th Hussars, having served as an armoured reconnaissance regiment with the Poles, was converted to DD swimming tanks—first Valentines and later Shermans. In the armoured divisions the 75mm Sherman had been virtually phased out in favour of the 76mm, 105mm, and 17pdr. variations, and they had been broken up into brigade and regimental groups each capable of operating with their own 'Kangaroo'-borne infantry, self-propelled artillery, specialized armour and 'Rover' air links with 'cab ranks' of fighter bombers. 8th Army advanced across the Senio River in April, and although the country was still awkward the armoured groups were in some cases able to make quite reasonable advances. Squadrons would move with troops in compact squares and infantry Kangaroos in close touch. Movement where possible was across country parallel to the roads, which were often mined and ambushed. At the same time the American 5th Army further west was pushing through the mountain passes towards Bologna.

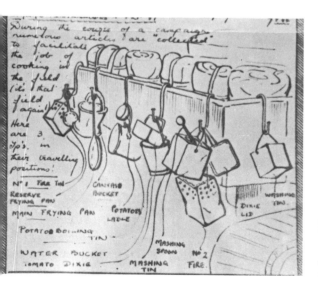

A special added rack for bedrolls, and an impressive array of cooking utensils, on the back of a Derbyshire Yeomanry Sherman. Many items were made from biscuit tins, since the advent of the jerrycan saw the end of the previous basic material for improvisation, the four-gallon petrol tin. Rear stowages of this type were convenient, and kept soot out of the tank, but one sometimes lost the lot when firing astern. (Cessford)

105mm Sherman IB of 9th Lancers in Italy. This tank has the cast nosepiece, 47° front plate with larger angled hatches, and the vision cupola for the commander.

The final key to the open plain and the Po Valley was the Argenta gap between Lake Comacchio and the River Reno. The plan for assaulting this heavily defended area included a commando landing from the lake, attacks by heavy bombers of the Strategic Air Force, various diversions and a set-piece attack making full use of the various 'Funnies'. The result was successful and the gap was forced by 15 April. Within another fortnight the Po had been reached, and the Germans were seeking surrender terms. (It was during this last phase of the fighting that perhaps the most bizarre Sherman casualty of the war occurred. A tank of 10th Hussars almost disappeared into a bomb crater filled with treacle, while fighting in a factory producing this sticky substance!)

Italy was the theatre of war which saw the longest and most diverse employment of the Sherman by the British Army, not to mention those of the Commonwealth and Allies; and despite the generally unsuitable terrain for armoured warfare, it was perhaps the area which gave the tank its best opportunity for showing its varied qualities in many different rôles.

North-West Europe

Although this is the campaign with which the Sherman is perhaps most readily associated, the tank's rôle here, at least as far as the British Army was concerned, was much narrower than in Italy. For a start the Tank Brigades were fully equipped with Churchills throughout, and the armoured Reconnaissance Regiments had the Cromwell Cruiser; then again, the need for tanks to double as artillery was much less, so the 105mm Sherman was not used. The greater availability of Fireflies also meant that comparatively few (if any) 76mms were used. Apart from the specialized conversions in 79th Armoured Division, there were only six brigades equipped with Shermans; two each in two of the three armoured divisions (7th had Cromwells instead, but did have Fireflies) and the others independent or 'swinger' brigades. This proportion of the British tank force was further reduced when one of the independent brigades was disbanded, another converted to specialized armour, and 11th Armoured Division gave up its Shermans and replaced them with the British Comet heavy Cruiser at the start of 1945. This is, of course, only the British picture; American and Canadian formations were virtually all equipped with Shermans throughout the campaign.

By D-Day the armoured regiments had various Marks of 75mm gun Shermans and up to a quarter of their strength of 17pdr. Fireflies. Those regiments in the assault brigades initially equipped with DD swimming tanks were all 75mms, but the non-swimming units had Fireflies. As time progressed the percentage of Fireflies was increased with availability until some regiments were only using 75mms as a support troop in squadron HQs.

For the actual D-Day landings on 6 June 1944, two brigades of Shermans, in which two of the three regiments of each had two squadrons equipped with DD tanks, landed in the van of the assault and, assisted by 79th Armoured Division's 'Funnies', helped the infantry to get ashore and breach the actual coastal defences. 8th Armoured Brigade worked with 50th Infantry Division on the westernmost 'Gold' beach, while 27th Armoured Brigade fought with 3rd Infantry Division to the east on 'Sword' (the two being separated by the Canadians on 'Juno'). Despite the fact that the weather delayed the DDs and made it necessary to land some of them dry-shod, the availability of gun tanks right up with the initial assault did much to assure its success.

After D-Day the struggle to enlarge and eventually break out from the bridgehead was to continue until the end of August, and was to be, in the opinion of one tank commander in Guards Armoured Division who fought the whole campaign in Shermans, the toughest fighting for armour they were to see (see Vanguard 9, *British Guards Armoured Division*). The remaining British armour was mostly ashore by the end of June. This gave 2nd Army six brigades of Shermans, one of Cromwells, and three tank brigades of Churchills, as well as the 'Funnies'.

During the initial fighting in the close Normandy country the Sherman was not an unqualified success: the 75mm was inadequate to take on Tigers and Panthers even at close ranges, vision was bad unless the commander risked death from snipers by fighting 'head out'; and compared with the Churchill, cross-country mobility was not good. In addition the armour was not proof against the heavier enemy tank and anti-tank guns (in some cases tanks were penetrated by shots that had already passed through a *bocage* field wall), and they brewed up easily and fast when hit. The British derivatives of the Culin prong device, which enabled Shermans to plough through field walls rather than climb over them, did not reach many units until too late to be of use. The limited number of Fireflies was adequate from the gun point of view; and despite heavy

Changing a damaged bogie wheel on a tank with the standard vertical volute suspension unit with trailing return roller. Bogies were one of the more vulnerable parts of the Sherman, but wheel units were relatively easy to change. Except in the desert, nearly all Shermans seem to have carried at least one spare bogie wheel, usually secured on the front plate.

The end in Italy: Shermans near Bologna. The farther of the two tanks is a command or OP vehicle with a fitted cable reel and extra aerials mounted on the hull; it also has a late-pattern turret with appliqué armour and a loader's hatch. The nearer has rubber block chevron tracks.

losses the high availability of Shermans enabled the British to wear down the Panzer formations, who could ill afford to lose the tanks they had, until the Americans were able to make the break-out to the west and south. Even the one major effort at more open warfare—Operation 'Goodwood'—while achieving its main objective of concentrating the Panzers against the British front, was a tactical failure; but this was due more to organizational and intelligence shortcomings than to the tanks with which the three participating armoured divisions were equipped.

When the break-out finally came, following the American sweep round from the west and the trapping of many of the German forces in Nor-

mandy in the Falaise pocket, the Sherman really came into its own, in perhaps the most favourable conditions that it was to meet throughout the entire war. While the Canadian Army on the coastal flank assaulted Le Havre, assisted by 33rd Armoured Brigade, and then the other channel ports, two corps of British 2nd Army advanced rapidly towards the Low Countries. XII Corps on the left, headed by 7th Armoured Division, made eventually for Ghent, with 4th Armoured Brigade acting as flank guard against bypassed enemy formations cut off along the coast; while XXX Corps launched 11th Armoured Division at Antwerp, and Guards Armoured followed up by 8th Armoured Brigade, at Brussels. The 1st and 3rd US Armies were advancing parallel and to the south. All these advances were made at continuous high speed against the scattered but, at times, determined resistance of self-propelled guns, 'bazookas', and the occasional enemy tank, arranged in small battlegroups. The process was very different from advances in the desert, as here whole divisions sometimes had to move along single roads with tanks, infantry and supporting arms judiciously arranged to enable quick and effective action when opposition was encountered. Although not quite as speedy as 7th Armoured Division's Cromwells (which at times outran their own wheeled transport even on the roads), the Shermans in the other formations amply demonstrated that given the space they could outclass the ponderous Tigers and unreliable Panthers in mobility, and thus largely negate their superiority in guns and armour except in ambush situations. Reliability once again played an important part in the success of the advance, and relatively few Shermans broke down, although some of the older ones which had developed excessive fuel consumptions ran dry. Brussels, Ghent and Antwerp were all entered during the first week in September, although the port at Antwerp was not to be opened for some time because of the enemy holding the River Scheldt further down. This had involved continuous marches of 40 to 50 miles a day, and since no major port had yet been put into use logistics forced a halt at this point.

It was to be 10 days before a further major assault could be launched, and this gave the

Germans time to recover somewhat and start to fight strongly and effectively amongst the dykes and canals of north Belgium and Holland. As a result, and because of less favourable terrain, the next move, Operation 'Market Garden', was to be a much tougher proposition. It started on 17 September with XXX Corps headed by Guards Armoured Division trying to make a narrow thrust right up to the Zuider Zee, to cut off the enemy in Holland and outflank the Ruhr. They had to race 60 miles up a single road axis across several major water obstacles, the bridges across which were to be captured in advance by the Allied Airborne Army.

As much of the road lay along embankments which it was impossible to move off, the tanks were almost sitting ducks and had to rely on massive air and artillery support, and close infantry co-operation, to get forward at all. It was a gamble that nearly came off; but the required depth of the advance, the delay in its start, the narrowness of the axis, the incomplete success of the airborne troops in capturing the bridges, and the unexpected presence of veteran Waffen-SS Panzer formations on the route all slowed and whittled away the armoured thrust, until it finally ran out of steam between Nijmegen and Arnhem on 21 September. Under the circumstances any tanks would have been at a disadvantage in this roadbound advance, and the Sherman, with its reliability, reasonable speed and ruggedness, was perhaps as well suited as any type, although the Cromwell might have moved faster, and the Churchill might have been better for the fighting in Nijmegen, if it had ever got there in time.

The winter of 1944–45 was a period of British and Canadian consolidation and preparation for the advance into Germany, while the three American armies to the south closed up to the Rhine. This did not give much scope for the British armoured formations, and mobility off the roads was severely curtailed for much of the time, despite the fitting of special end-connectors to increase the Sherman's track area. The operations to clear the Scheldt estuary and open up the port of Antwerp, on which further British advances depended, involved Canadian armour and 'Funnies', and while the German Ardennes offensive at Christmas caused much precaution-

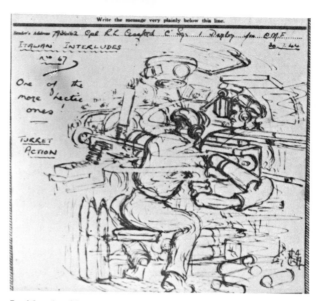

Inside the Sherman turret in action; and writing home during a quiet moment. The loader's glove was necessary to protect the hand when punching the round home, and when handling hot cases. The rounds stowed loose on the turret floor were common in Italy, and proved something of a hazard to the crew when the tank was bouncing over rough country. (Cessford)

ary scurrying about, it resulted in little action. (General Martel made some interesting speculations as to how the German advance through the difficult country might have been improved from its five or six miles a day had they been able to use Shermans and Cromwells rather than the monstrous King Tigers, etc.) The battle of the Reichswald, to break through the Siegfried Line and reach the Rhine, started very much as an infantry affair, with even the Churchills of the tank brigades having difficulty coping with the floods and mud. In consequence many armoured units spent much of the winter holding the line, sometimes even leaving their tanks and acting as impromptu infantry.

By the spring of 1945 only Guards Armoured Division and 4th and 8th Armoured Brigades were still equipped with Shermans. (27th Armoured Brigade had been disbanded after Normandy, 33rd was converting to Buffalo amphibians, and 11th Armoured Division now had its Comets.) The final phase of the war against Germany started with the crossing of the Rhine. This was a full-scale assault with airborne troops dropped on the far bank, infantry crossing in Buffaloes, and DD Shermans, as well as much air and artillery support, beefed up by 'pepperpots' fired by tanks and infantry weapons. The armoured brigades crossed by raft and Bailey bridge at the end of March as soon as the bridgehead was established. Guards Armoured Division and 8th Armoured Brigade in XXX Corps took the northern sector, with the Canadians on their left, while to the south XII Corps had 7th Armoured Division with its Cromwells, and 4th Armoured Brigade. After the initial crossings VIII Corps, which included 11th Armoured Division, joined in on the right flank, with the (now) four American Armies and one French Army to its south. The stiffest fighting occurred in the XXX Corps sector, and while the other corps were able to make speedy advances between isolated pockets of resistance, albeit many of them fierce, XXX Corps had to fight every inch of the way against the fanatical 1st Parachute Army, advancing over cratered roads and (almost invariably) blown bridges. By the start of May the Shermans were at the Elbe when the Germans finally surrendered; and although it was still to see active service elsewhere for many years, the Sherman tank in all its many forms had completed its major contribution to the British war effort.

Loading for the invasion of North-West Europe. Waterproofed Shermans of 13th/18th Hussars, 27th Armoured Brigade, reversing into a Landing Craft Tank at Gosport in June 1944. The smaller LCTs carried the assault waves of tanks while the larger LSTs brought in the follow-up waves once the beach was empty.

Burma

The conditions and type of fighting in the Far East were different yet again, and since the Japanese had neither effective tanks nor anti-tank guns the need for a 'modern' tank such as the Sherman was less acute than elsewhere. Grants and Lees, Stuarts, and even Australian Matildas proved adequate throughout the theatre as a whole; but by 1943 Shermans were becoming the most readily available tanks and some Indian Army units began to receive them. Although there were no British armoured formations in Burma, two Indian tank brigades each had a British regiment in them, as was Indian Army custom. The 3rd Carabiniers in 254 Brigade kept their Lees and Grants until the end of the war, so do not concern us here (again, see Vanguard 6); but in 255 Brigade, 116 Regiment, Royal Armoured Corps (converted from 9th Gordon Highlanders, a territorial infantry unit) had Shermans. Although small in comparison with the moves of divisions and brigades of Shermans in other theatres, their activities make an interesting comparison with which to round off the British Sherman's 'active service' story.

116 Regt. RAC was organized as a 52-tank regiment, all Shermans, mostly Mark Vs but including some Mark Is. A full complement of 75mm tanks was kept throughout the campaign, there being no call for the more specialized armaments needed elsewhere. They first went into action in January 1945 when 255 Indian Tank Brigade made a 200-mile march on their own tracks (the roads being too bad for transporters) to cross the Irrawaddy so as to capture Meiktila and cut off Mandalay from the south. In the event the 116th spent nearly six weeks fighting in the bridgehead and laying on diversionary attacks while the rest of the brigade and other arms went for Meiktila itself. The CO of 116 RAC only remembers encountering enemy tanks once and being attacked by aircraft on three occasions during the whole campaign. The fighting was very much in the 'I' tank rôle, and often involved blasting open concealed bunkers so that the infantry could capture them. A drill for this was devised using successive rounds of HE, to strip

Sherman DD in action ashore. The flotation screen has been collapsed and partly cut away to give a field of fire to the 'lap' gun. Spare sprockets, track-plates and sandbags have been ingeniously arranged to give added frontal protection. It does not seem to have been a very general practice for the crew's packs to be hung around the turret, but this tank has a neat stowage rail added.

away the vegetation and camouflage; smoke, to conceal the infantry while they closed up on the target; and solid shot to break it open, all from ranges of down to a few yards. The main enemy of the tanks were suicidal infantry tank-hunting parties with grenades and explosive charges, who would literally board the tanks if given the chance. In close country the Shermans were very vulnerable to this mode of attack, and the brigade had an 'escort battalion' of Bombay Grenadiers to give close protection to them, in place of the 'motor battalions' used in other theatres.

After the fall of Meiktila, 116 RAC (with the rest of 255 Brigade) was formed into columns with infantry, self-propelled field artillery, and other supporting arms, to make up the armoured spearhead of the easternmost of the two attacks launched south towards Rangoon. In this rôle they completed a highly successful advance of 300 miles down the Sittang Valley, racing to reach Rangoon before the monsoon broke, in just three weeks. At one point they were sufficiently in advance of enemy intelligence to find a Japanese military policeman trying to direct the leading tanks, only to be run down for his pains. Mopping up continued after the fall of Rangoon and some Shermans of 116 RAC were still in action a week after the war ended, subduing unbelieving 'Sons of Heaven', and thus being the very last armoured unit in action in that war.

Sherman II of 3rd CLY fitted with the Culin prong device for cutting through *bocage* hedgerows. Many British units received these too late to be of much use. This tank is typically stowed for North-West Europe, with gear fore and aft but the sides clear. (Sharpshooters)

Although older types of tank were still able to hold their own in Burma the Sherman once again proved a success, due to its reliability under adverse conditions and the extreme accuracy of its gun, which was of particular value for 'posting' rounds into the firing slits of bunkers. It thus enhanced the reputation for versatility gained in North Africa, Italy and North-West Europe.

The Sherman Remembered

It is not easy to make an overall assessment of a tank. The official 'facts' are often based on workshop trials of new vehicles and range tests of weapons under ideal conditions; likewise, official accounts of performance in action can be misleading due to the natural tendency to play down the weak points of one's own equipment and stress the good ones, while doing the reverse for that of the enemy, not only for public propaganda purposes but also to bolster the morale of one's own troops. On the other hand the impressions of combat crews, if taken from a reasonably wide

cross-section of units, can give many insights into what a tank was really like; but these, too, must be treated with caution, as memories are fickle, and in some cases myths or traditions based on isolated incidents, or faulty understanding at the time, have been handed down as generally applicable fact. Published works tend to concentrate on particularly 'popular' campaigns and battles, so unless a comprehensive range of material is consulted these can also give a false impression — in the case of the Sherman, for example, that its relatively unsatisfactory performance in Normandy against static Tigers and Panthers gives a valid example of its overall usefulness. It is hoped that the previous chapters of this book, describing the full range of campaigns in which it fought in British service during the Second World War, have conveyed a suitably balanced overall view; but it remains to go to the other end of the scale, and to see what was thought of the Sherman by those who fought in it.

This composite view of the tank, giving its strengths and its weaknesses, has been compiled from a series of interviews with ex-Sherman crew members backed up by comments in unit and formation histories and wartime training pamphlets. Although obviously not exhaustive, a fairly comprehensive range of individual experience has been drawn upon. Those interviewed included the curator and librarian of the RAC Tank Museum at Bovington (with Sherman experience in RTR units in Italy); the commanding officer of 116 Regt. RAC (Burma); officers of 3 and 3/4 County of London Yeomanry (North Africa, Italy and North-West Europe), and Staffordshire Yeomanry (desert and North-West Europe—DDs and Fireflies); a driver, a sergeant tank commander and a unit fitter of 10th Hussars (North Africa and Italy); a sergeant tank commander of Grenadier Guards (North-West Europe), a corporal operator of 51 RTR (Sherman in 'I' tank rôle in Italy) and a corporal driver/co-driver, and later tank commander, of Notts. (Sherwood Rangers) Yeomanry (DD and gun tanks, North-West Europe). The first thing that becomes clear is that on some points users' views were almost unanimous, whereas on others they differed widely. In many cases these differences can be traced to differing conditions in the various theatres of war, and in others to the previous service experience of the men or units concerned, which coloured their views of the Sherman.

One matter on which there seems to have been general agreement was the excellence of the Sherman's armament. Compared with the 2pdr. and 6pdr. and the short 75mm of the Grant, the 75mm M3 gun was a fine all-round weapon. (The guns from scrapped Shermans in North Africa were even fitted as a local modification to Churchills, then designated NA75s.) Its relatively poor AP performance seems only to have been considered a serious disadvantage in North-West Europe. In Italy and the Far East its extreme accuracy, its simplicity and reliability, and its effective HE performance more than outweighed its lack of penetration, since heavy enemy armour was not the main opponent in those areas; and AP performance was adequate against enemy tanks met in the desert. There the Sherman 75mm was officially considered a more effective means of destroying anti-tank guns than were infantry attacks. It could successfully engage such targets at up to 2,000 yards, and even when they were concealed the blast from a concentration of 75mm HE rounds would often strip away camouflage and enable them to be pinpointed and killed.

After Alamein techniques were perfected for firing indirect with an observer off the tank, artillery style, and semi-indirect with the tank 'turret down' behind cover with the commander observing, standing on the turret top if necessary. This method of fire was used with AP as well as HE and smoke, and at Alamein one unit was credited with five enemy tanks for an expenditure of six rounds each, the AP shot plunging down through the thin top armour. This was possibly a tank of the 10th Hussars, who are known to have used this technique while supporting the Rifle Brigade action at Snipe, and who had the benefit of an attached Belgian artillery officer who had served with the famous '75' of the First World War, to train them; most units do not seem to have become

Sherman II of 44 RTR refuelling shortly after landing in Normandy. The lower part of the exhaust trunk fitted for wading ashore is still in place. The turret bin is the simple flat-topped type used in North-West Europe. Coamings have been welded on either side aft to retain stowed gear.

expert at such methods until rather later in the campaign. To enable simple spotting corrections to be made the elevating and traversing handwheels had a number of divisions inscribed around the rim and a marker to line them up with; later, azimuth indicators were fitted.

On some occasions in Italy Shermans were used for considerable periods as artillery from properly surveyed positions, using paraphernalia such as artillery boards and gunner's quadrants on the gun breeches. One squadron on the River Lamone fired 6,000 rounds in a fortnight in this rôle; it was estimated that the 75mm could fire 100 rounds per hour for two hours without overheating, or one round every two minutes almost indefinitely. (As a matter of interest, statistics show that the average number of rounds fired by a Sherman during its *life* was ten!) More usual, however, were impromptu shoots, either by a single tank, or by a troop or squadron firing together. A system of multiple bracketing was sometimes used where the squadron second-in-command or troop leader would get his rounds falling near the target and then order the other tanks to put the same handwheel settings on their guns, the whole lot being boldly corrected after each salvo to bracket the target and reduce the errors until hits were obtained. The M48 HE ammunition had a .05 second delay that could be set, and this was used on occasion to produce airbursts from ricochets. Apart from occasions during battles such as the Reichswald, indirect fire was less widely used in North-West Europe, although unobserved 'pepperpots' were employed to cover river crossings and the like. Direct fire was also very much the norm in Burma. The 75mm was extremely accurate in this rôle, although the sights had to be checked and aligned daily to keep it so, and they suffered from considerable refraction light loss. In some units slight play in them was taken up by wedging with strips of paper or a cigarette carton; in the later M34A1 gun mounting a telescope sight was added. In Burma special commander's sights, consisting of a pivoted arm with sight rings on a quadrant, were manufactured locally and fastened to the blade sighting vanes on the top of the turret, but the exact method of their use is no longer clear.

Opinions on the 105mm gun, fitted in some HQ tanks in Italy, vary. Its smoke round was much admired, and many units became expert in its use with HE, engaging targets with it at up to five miles, but others reckoned that its use of variable charges made it too complicated for a tank weapon. Despite its fairly general adoption the 76mm does not seem to have been universally popular either, probably due to drawbacks with the turret and the fact that its extra AP performance was not much needed in Italy, while its higher velocity and flatter trajectory made it a less accurate HE weapon than the 75mm. Neither was the 17pdr. in the Firefly a great success with HE, since it had little ammunition for this rôle, and observation from it was often impossible due to the dust kicked up by its muzzle blast, apart from loss of accuracy due to its flat trajectory. For AP work, however, it was the only answer to the heavier German armour and so became justifiably popular in North-West Europe (where one regiment had been forced to ram their first Royal Tiger as the 75mm would not penetrate it even at point-blank range). The 75mm, 76mm, and 17pdr. all fired APC and APCBC rounds, but the APDS round which became available for the 17pdr. in 1945 seems to have been mainly issued to anti-tank units. Main armament firing was almost always carried out stopped, and it is difficult to find anyone who remembers ever using the stabilizer for firing on the move.

The Browning .30 cal. co-axial and 'lap' (hull) guns were frequently used on the move for 'prophylactic fire', spraying roadside hedgerows or surrounding jungle, and in some cases the smoke mortars were used to fire 2in. infantry HE mortar bombs for the same purpose. The Browning seems to have been much more popular than the British Besa, with its reputation for frequent stoppages, although one unit found that all its Brownings wore out at the same time. The cumbersome .50 cal. provided as an AA machine gun was less well liked, and was often not mounted except in harbour. Complaints range from its liability to catch in the vines in Italy, to that of one CLY tank commander who had to cower in his turret when the ammunition belt was hit, providing a most uncomfortable firework display. Some crews preferred to try and engage low fliers with

continued on page 26

1. Sherman II, 'B' Sqn., Staffordshire Yeomanry; El Alamein, 1942
2. Sherman II, 'B' Sqn., Wiltshire Yeomanry; El Alamein, 1942
a. Unit tacsign, Staffordshire Yeomanry   b. 10th Armoured Division
c. 2nd NZ Division; Wiltshire Yeomanry tacsign; and 9th Armoured Brigade

MICHAEL ROFFE

A

1. Sherman I, HQ 4th Armoured Brigade; Sicily, 1943
a. 4th Armoured Brigade

2. Sherman I, 'A' Sqn., 3rd County of London Yeomanry
Sicily, 1943

1. Sherman IIA, 'A' Sqn., 10th Royal Hussars; Italy, 1944

2. Sherman V of CO, 116 Regt. RAC; Burma, 1945
a. 1st Armoured Division b. 7th Armoured Division
c. 11th Armoured Division d. Guards Armoured Division

MICHAEL ROFFE

C

1. Sherman V of CO, 1st (Armoured)
Coldstream Guards; Holland, 1944

2. Sherman I, '1' Sqn., 2nd (Armoured)
Irish Guards, Normandy, 1944

D

MICHAEL ROFFE

1. Sherman DD, 13th/18th Royal Hussars; Normandy, 1944

1

2. Sherman V, RHQ 13th/18th Royal Hussars; Normandy, 1944

2

MICHAEL ROFFE

E

Sherman VC Firefly turret interior, looking forward; see key on page 25, and Plates commentary.

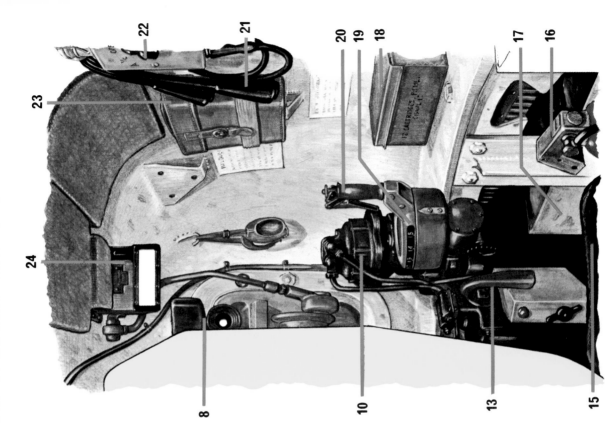

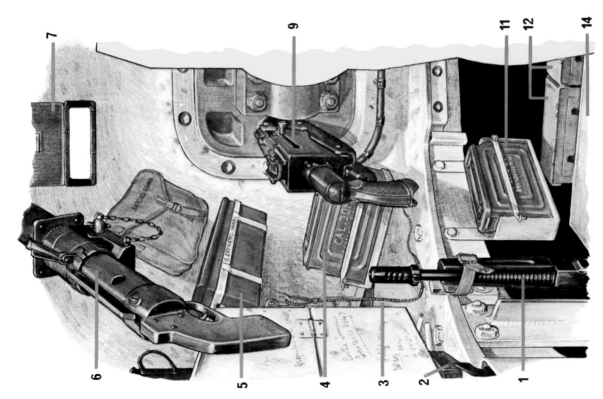

F

MIKE CHAPPELL

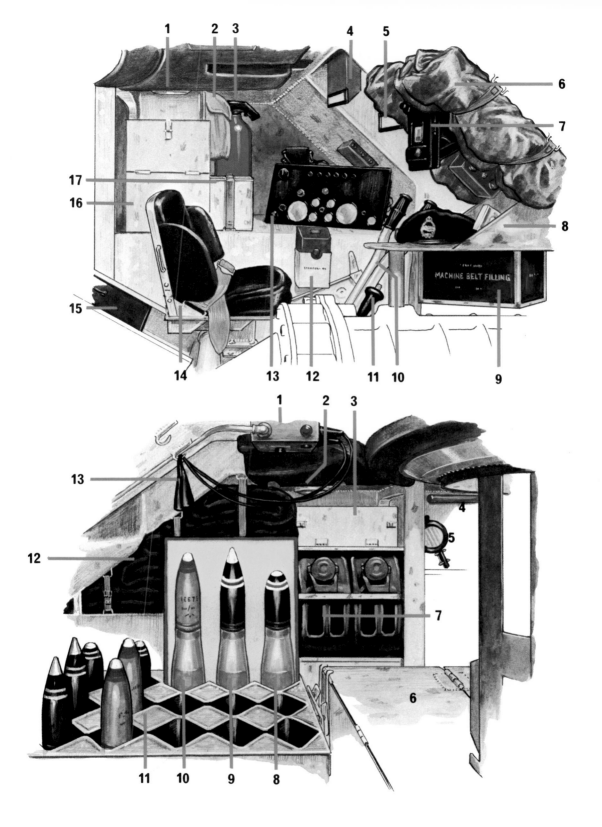

Sherman VC Firefly driver's position; and ammunition stowage in right front hull position. See key on page 25, and Plates commentary.

G

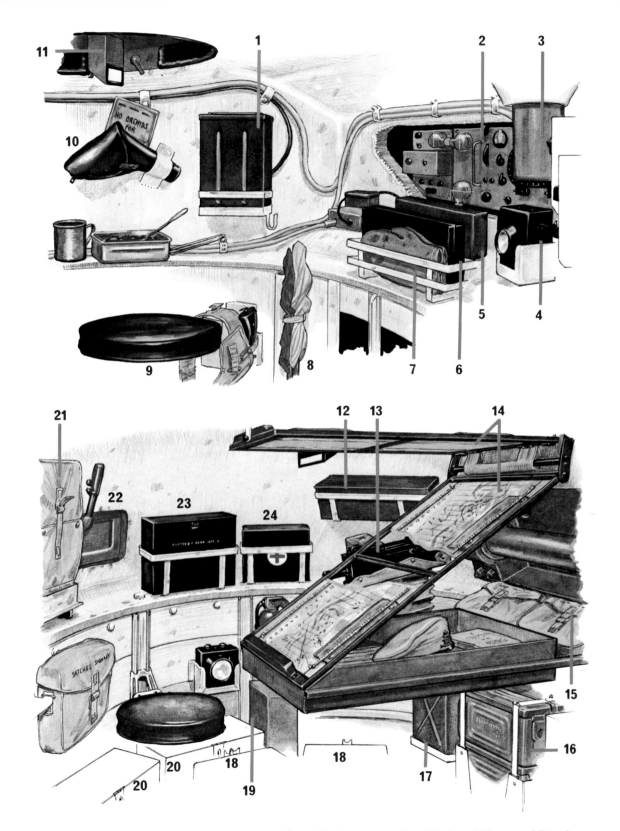

Sherman VC Firefly turret interior, looking right and back, gun breech omitted; and Sherman OP tank turret interior, looking left and forward. See key on page 25, and Plates commentary.

H

MIKE CHAPPEL

Key, Plate F: Sherman VC Firefly turret interior, looking forward, with gun breech omitted:

Perspective is necessarily slightly distorted, and the space left by the omitted 17pdr. breech and recoil shield would in fact be much wider in proportion.

1 Thompson sub-machine gun
2 MG ruptured cartridge extractor
3 Cocking lanyard for .30 cal. Browning co-axial MG
4 250 rds. ammunition, .30 cal., in feed tray
5 Six hand grenades
6 2in. bomb-thrower
7 Mk.6 periscope
8 Gunner's brow pad and sighting telescope
9 Co-axial .30 cal. Browning MG
10 Power traverse
11 Stowage, 250 rds. ammunition, .30 cal.
12 Stowage, eight 2in. smoke bombs
13 Power traverse spade grip
14 Stowage, 3rds. for 17pdr. gun
15 Gunner's seat
16 4lb. CO² fire extinguisher
17 Right hand sponson bin holding cleaning, maintenance and tool kits, crew haversacks and groundsheets, and general stowage.
18 Twelve flare cartridges
19 Traverse indicator
20 Hand traverse
21 Headset drop leads
22 Commander's radio selection box—A, B, or intercom.
23 Binocular case
24 Mk.4 periscope

Plate G (top): Sherman VC Firefly driver's position, looking left:

1 Light
2 Signals satchel
3 4lb. CO² fire extinguisher
4 Mk.6 periscope
5 Direct vision visor
6 Gas capes
7 Compass pioneer
8 Driver's hatch hood stowage, usually used for small kit
9 MG belt-filling device in chest
10 Track steering levers
11 Gear change lever
12 Spare Mk.6 periscope
13 Instrument panel, with goggles and water bottles stowed behind
14 Seat with safety harness
15 .50 cal. MG ammunition stowage chest
16 Stowage for vehicle tools, fuel funnel, wire, tape, spare bulbs etc.
17 Stowage, spare Mk.6 periscope and three heads

Plate G (bottom): Sherman VC Firefly right hand hull position, looking right:

1 Intercom box
2 Light
3 Stowage for Colman cooker, and twelve biscuit tins
4 Stowage for antennae rods
5 Spare headlight stowage
6 Stowage for 20 rds, 17pdr. gun
7 Stowage, two 5-gal. water cans
8 These three 17pdr. rounds have been artificially 'pulled up' out of their stowage and set against a yellow background, to show their relative length.
9
10 17pdr. round, Armour Piercing Capped (APC)
9 17pdr. round, Armour Piercing Capped, Ballistic Cap (APCBC)
10 17pdr. round, High Explosive Mk.1 T
11 Stowage, 15 rds. for 17pdr. gun
12 Stowage, twelve blankets
13 Headset drop leads

Plate H (top): Sherman VC Firefly turret interior, looking right and to rear, with gun breech omitted:

1 Stowage, 50 rds. ammunition, .50 cal.
2 No.19 Set
3 Variometer
4 Hellesen hand lamp
5 Ten magazines for Sten SMG, or 22 for Thompson SMG
6 First aid kit
7 Two pairs asbestos mittens
8 Tank distinguishing flags
9 Commander's seat
10 Signal pistol
11 Commander's hatch with Mk.6 periscope

Plate H (bottom): Sherman artillery OP tank turret interior, looking left and forward:

12 Six hand grenades
13 Co-axial .30 cal. Browning MG retained, with ammo box in feed tray, and spent cartridge bag below.
14 Four map boards in swivelling mountings, two by two—yellow line indicates cutaway to show MG.
15 Signals satchels
16 Stowage, seven 250-rd. boxes, .30 cal. ammo
17 Stowage chest, .50 cal. ammo
18 Two 50-rd. boxes, .50 cal. ammo
19 Stowage, Mk.6 periscope and three spare heads
20 Stowage, six No.8 smoke generators
21 No.18 Set
22 Pistol port
23 Stowage, spare batteries
24 First aid kit

25

Headquarters, 29th Armoured Brigade, 11th Armoured Division. The command tank (right) is an elderly Sherman I with vision slits and the narrow M34 gun mantlet. Steps have been welded to the three-piece nose casting to facilitate the ascent of senior officers, and there are at least two aerials mounted on the hull as well as the normal ones on the turret, and a cable reel. The scout cars are Humbers.

the co-axial by swinging the turret, but in fairness the need for AA defence was much decreased by the time the Sherman saw most of its action. Some units continued to mount an AA machine gun, however, a .30 cal. sometimes being used in place of the .50 cal., and Corporal Charlton of the Irish Guards won a posthumous v.c. using the one from his tank in the ground rôle in Germany. Shermans were not equipped with the electric smoke generators that British Cruisers mounted, but the 2in. mortars and 4in. dischargers with which they were fitted (except apparently in the Far East) were popular, as was the ability to fire smoke from the main gun. By 1944 the bulky Thompson guns with which crews were issued had mostly been replaced by the smaller but more

temperamental Stens; grenades were much used in close country, and those crew members who still wore their personal revolvers (many did not) seem to have preferred the ordinary belt holster to the RAC variety with leg strap, when they could get them.

Another point on which there seems to be general agreement was the high degree of mechanical reliability of the Sherman, and its ease of maintenance compared with British-made tanks, at least up to late 1944. Of the types in British service the Mark III, with its two General Motors diesels, was undoubtedly the favourite, and no-one seems to be able to remember any regular snags with it, except for occasional overheating. Next came the Mark V with the Chrysler multibank. This could suffer loss of power if the timing failed and one or more banks went out of synchronization with the rest; it was sometimes prone to petrol stoppages, and initially, when the carburettors were mounted individually on each of the five engines, the bottom two tended to

The M3 75mm gun in its M34A1 combination mount being lifted out of a Sherman in Burma. The co-axial Browning has already been removed from the mounting, and the 'lap' gun is not fitted in this tank, which has had additional armour welded in front of the co-driver's hatch; from the chip taken out of it, this was probably just as well!

flood. This was later cured by mounting them all in a bank at the top, and despite its complexity this was still basically a very reliable power unit. The original Whirlwind radial-engined Marks I and II were the least popular. The lower plugs were awkward to get at unless the engine was lifted out, and because of the height of the tank and lack of a special derrick this involved jacking up the back of a Scammell to provide a crane and could take the best part of a day. As with the earlier American radials, the engine had to be hand-turned before starting if it had been standing for any time, to avoid a vapour lock in the bottom cylinders. The air filters were poorly placed and clogged up with a cement of sand and oil every 25 miles or so in the desert, and the clutch was rather awkward to get at to grease, but apart from these fairly minor snags the Shermans would run continuously for 50 miles a day with no trouble. Routine maintenance only took about an hour a

night, which compared favourably with the time taken for the British Cruisers, or to grease the numerous bogies on the Churchill.

The Sherman was also simple to drive, and although requiring strength was less tiring to drive than many types, and had a more comfortable driver's seat than British tanks. The fact that skid turns were not possible with the controlled differential steering system (although good drivers could virtually achieve them in bottom gear) was not found to be a serious disadvantage in service, and was more than outweighed by the simplicity and reliability resulting from having the driver on top of the steering gear, with the driving sprockets at the front of the tank. Mechanically the Sherman had few vices and survived neglect better than more sophisticated machines, although, as with other American tanks, the use of US screwthreads sometimes caused problems for unit fitters with their British 1927 tool-kits. The tanks were in fact provided with a very good tool-kit, but being an attractive item this was all too often missing by the time they reached units. The bogies were one of the more vulnerable components, but there was a special tool that made changing them relatively easy.

Although larger and more roomy than most British tanks, the larger gun and ammunition, particularly in the Fireflies, still left the turret fairly cramped; but it was possible to 'brew up' inside and there were instances of live chickens being kept in the driver's compartment! Proper petrol cookers were provided, but many ex-desert crews preferred to use earth and petrol 'Benghazis' right to the end of the war. Internal stowage was much more lavish than in British tanks, with a place for everything even down to water-bottles and highly attractive torches—provided with typical American thoroughness. Some crews thought this was overdone and resulted in too much clutter inside, but many appreciated it. The bulky ammunition had to be handed around the tank to the loader once the first few rounds were used, and fumes were a problem when shut down and firing; but since more than four or five rounds were seldom fired at a time, and the empty cases were ditched through the pistol port, this was not too much of a problem. The canvas bag beneath the gun for the used cartridge cases was frequently dispensed with as the gun might not eject properly and might jam if it became topped up. In some cases in Italy extra ammunition stowages were made from the cylindrical cases in which the rounds were supplied, and were fastened in the sponsons and under the gun; in others, extra rounds were carried loose on the turret floor. In general the tank was reasonably comfortable despite a perpetual draught through the turret with the radial-engined Marks, and a very hot driver's compartment in warm climes, due to the transmission being at the front, which sometimes caused shrapnel casualties due to the hatches being left open for ventilation, however stern the orders.

External stowages, as with all tanks, were hardly adequate. In most areas bins were fastened to the backs of turrets, or in the case of Firefles with their extended turrets, specially designed ones were fitted to the hull rear plate, or even sometimes the hull front. In the Far East turret bins were not used, but a flat 'tray' was fitted on top of the engine deck, and water *chagals* were sometimes slung around the turret. Bedding was often secured under the tarpaulin on the rear end of the engine deck, where it got nice and warm (tinned food was also sometimes stowed on the grilles beside the exhausts to give a hot meal immediately on stopping), but the sloping rear decks of the Sherman were not as suitable for stowage as the flatter ones of some other types. To combat this some units welded metal coamings around the back corners. In the desert spare kit was slung from the side rails fitted for the 'sunshade' lorry camouflage; but in Sicily and Italy, although many tanks still had

Sherman V following Sherman I of 144 Regt. RAC in 33rd Armoured Brigade. As was the case with many regiments in North-West Europe the tanks are numbered consecutively throughout, so these are of 'B' Squadron. On the original print the green-over-black 'diabolo' brigade sign (it was previously a Tank Brigade) can just be made out on the left rear; and the regimental tacsign, 174 on red, is on the first aid box, partly obscured by the field telephone slung at the right rear.

the rails, this was discontinued as gear tended to get torn off on roadside trees and other obstacles. Thereafter the sloping hull front and front track-guards became popular, with empty ammunition boxes welded on to make impromptu lockers. A field telephone was sometimes attached to the back plate to provide a 'house phone' for infantry to communicate with the tank commander— supposing he could hear them above the noise of the engine; this later became a proper fixture on British tanks.

The fact that the Sherman was not impervious to the heavier enemy anti-tank projectiles seems to have caused more comment from those coming from Churchills, or not having previously served in the flimsier British Cruisers, than from experienced armoured regiment crews, who noticed the improvement on previous types and did not really expect anything to keep out an '88'. Extra plates were officially added over sensitive areas (being welded on, ironically, by German prisoners of war in some units), and old trackplates or sandbags were sometimes used for extra protection, but apart from North-West Europe such improvisations were not much used. In a few isolated

Sherman Firefly of 'A' Sqn., Staffordshire Yeomanry shortly after landing in Normandy. The square giving dimensional details of the tank is still painted in the centre of the box across the hull front. The small squadron and unit tacsigns just visible below it in the centre of the lower hull front are typical of the brigade; in this regiment the 27th Armoured Brigade sign of the seahorse, better known as the 'pregnant pilchard', and the 3rd Infantry Division sign of the 'Bass' red triangle were sometimes seen on either side of these.

cases sheets of boiler plate were fixed in front of the hull front plate to counteract the various hollow-charge infantry weapons of 'bazooka' type, and in Burma angle-iron frames and wire netting were fastened over engine decks and hull fronts to prevent magnetic or sticky charges being attached. In some cases the Sherman's best form of defence was attack, and the Firefly at least could often stalk the ponderous Tigers with success, due to their slow turret traverse and unmanoeuvrability.

The Sherman's evil reputation for brewing up or even exploding within a matter of seconds when penetrated was subject to various opinions as to cause. The official explanation was that the high and poorly protected ammunition stowages made the cartridges liable to be punctured and ignited by splinters; with the size and number of

Sherman V of 24th Lancers in France. The combined 8th Armoured Brigade sign (fox's mask), over unit tacsign (995 on red) with a white bar beneath to identify it as an independent 'Army' brigade, is on the left of the hull backplate.

rounds carried the chances of touching one off must certainly have been high. One commander tells of the base plates shearing off 75mm rounds under the impact of a hit on the hull, spewing loose cordite out into the turret; but another describes finding cartridges charred but intact inside a burnt-out Sherman. A popular scapegoat was the high-octane petrol used in the radial-engined Marks, and a comment that there was always a smell of petrol in the turrets of these tanks suggests the possibility of sparks causing a flash-back and explosion; but the similarly fuelled Stuarts and Grants do not seem to have had the same unsavoury reputation, and at least one tank commander interviewed was sure that the diesel-engined tanks brewed more readily than the petrol ones. Another interesting suggestion was that they seldom brewed if hit in the front.

Anyway, it is beyond dispute that if hit the crew often had little time to bale out, and all seem to have been very conscious of this. Some tell of removing all clips from the hatches to avoid any

danger of their sticking in the shut position; and with the earlier Marks with only one turret hatch, one unit at least unofficially removed the gun recoil guards to allow the loader to get across to the hatch more easily—but they admit this resulted in at least one set of broken ribs when someone got in the way when the gun was fired. In other instances one flap of the turret hatch, or the circular lid of the cupola on the 76mm turret, was removed altogether. Although considered less easy to bale out from than the Churchill with its large side doors, or the Grant, there were fewer positions in which the turret could jam the driver's hatches than in the early Cromwells, and the Sherman did have an escape hatch in the hull floor behind the co-driver. This was originally an inspection plate, but was soon kept unbolted as a matter of course (one driver remembers seeing another tank's plate fall open in action, scattering kit and brewing gear onto the sand as it went along) and was then modified so that it could be knocked out with a hammer, fitted in a special stowage for the purpose.

Concealment and camouflage points peculiar to the Sherman were few, but Fireflies sometimes had collars fitted part-way along the gun barrel, and the forward length painted white to give the impression of a shorter gun, and thus hopefully to avoid preferential treatment from enemy anti-tank guns. A 10th Hussar also remembers having open-ended tubes welded along the hull sides for sticking branches in, but this does not seem to have been a general practice. One official report stresses the need for camouflage when on the move at night, to break up the vehicle's silhouette. From a concealment point of view the Sherman's worst feature was its height; this was particularly so in the desert, due to the difficulty of finding good hull-down positions for it. Another drawback resulting from the tank's height became apparent in Italy—it was top-heavy, particularly when fitted with the heavier T23 type of turret for the 76mm gun. This caused considerable anxiety among crews about turning over when travelling on narrow roads where one side might collapse under the weight of a tank, or when moving across a slope, where a shell bursting under the uphill

side could topple it. One regiment had a tank roll right over on a hillside, landing on its tracks still in gear and running on, albeit with a badly-shaken crew.

Markings were of course the same as used on other types of tank, but the relatively large surface areas of the turrets and hull sides gave plenty of scope for those units that went in for large-size signs, as several did in North-West Europe. Many of the crews did not know at the time what the various tactical and other signs meant, and it is rare today to find anyone who can remember them in detail. One widely-used sign not perhaps obvious from photographs was the yellow fabric

Re-ammunitioning a Firefly with 17pdr. APCBC rounds. Wire netting with hessian/foliage camouflage on turret and gun barrel only was fairly common in Normandy, where field banks and hedges usually concealed the hull, and anything attached to it tended to get stripped off by the vegetation when moving across country.

'Crock' a Sherman II of 'C' Sqn., 3rd CLY; in this unit tank names began with squadron letters. The crew wear winter tank suits. The unit tacsign (123 on red) and 4th Armoured Brigade sign (black jerboa on white) are just visible in the original print on the right and left final drive housings respectively. (Sharpshooters)

square, with tapes for securing it to the turret top, which was a standard air recognition sign. Little faith seems to have been placed in the roundels or stars, and some say they painted them out.

In common with most tanks of the period visibility was not good when shut down, and most armoured unit tank commanders continued to fight 'head out', in many cases also scorning the use of steel helmets, even in Normandy, where sniping and such horrors as mines suspended from trees were serious hazards. 'I' tank units, and Shermans in Burma, do seem to have fought shut down as a rule. The cupola fitted on the 76mm T23 turret was something of an improvement and some liked it, although others reckoned its only advantage was to enable one to drive shut down when it was raining; one commander said that the only personal weapon needed in Italy was an umbrella. The exposed glassware was liable to catch the sun and reveal a tank's position, so was sometimes kept greased over. The British-type vision cupola, used on later Churchills and Comets, which was fitted to a few Shermans at

the end of the war, had the top windows of the episcopes better shielded.

The size of the Sherman turret allowed considerable flexibility in communication fits. Gun tanks could at a pinch fit two No. 19 sets, allowing a squadron net and rear link to be maintained in the same vehicle if required, or a 19 and an infantry 38 set could be fitted. Command tanks in some cases fitted as many as four 19 sets with the gun removed (and found the redundant ammunition racks handy for bottles of vino). Opinions varied as to the usefulness of having an infantry set; some fitted and used them, others had squadron second captains moving on foot with the infantry to tell them what the tanks were up to, and some squadron COs actually carried deckchairs on their engine decks for the infantry commander, so they could talk face to face. What the infantry thought of this rather exposed method of communication is not recorded. Apart from some comments that the 'B' set (troop intercom) was unreliable, and early troubles in the desert with 19 sets overheating due to a design fault, communications seem to have worked well, although for much of the Sherman's service they were only required to cope with relatively short ranges. The provision of portable charging engines helped to solve the problem of flat batteries during static periods.

The cross-country mobility of the Sherman was generally agreed to be adequate, but opinions varied as to how good it was and how it compared with that of other tanks. Some thought that it was better than the Crusader with its Christie suspension, despite giving a rougher ride, on account of its better tracks and greater ground clearance; others disagreed. In North-West Europe, where much running was done on roads, the rubber chevron tracks were generally popular, but in Italy the metal chevron or cleated types seem to have been much preferred. Likewise in North-West Europe use was made of the extended end connectors to increase track area in winter, whereas in Italy resort was made to the 'Platypus' grouser (the ordinary grousers seem seldom to have been used on British Shermans). With Platypus grousers on every second or third link many reckoned that the Sherman could go almost anywhere, but unlike the extended end connectors they could not be used all the time, as they

reduced road speeds to about 2½mph; and since they extended out beyond the sides of the hull they were prone to snag roadside obstacles and made the tank too wide to use Bailey bridges. They also chewed up unmade roads; one unit made a practice of having a tankdozer travelling in reverse at the tail of the column dragging its dozer blade to conceal the damage they did. In addition to all this a set of Platypus took about eight hours to fit or remove.

DD swimming tanks of course had their own particular problems. Apart from swamping in rough seas (when the crew were supposed to escape using DSEA sets of the type which the Navy abandoned after the war in favour of free-ascent submarine escape techniques) they were difficult to steer and drifted rapidly in any current.

REME Sherman ARV Mark I, towing a captured PzKpfw IV. These early ARVs had snatchblocks, tow ropes, and a light jib for engine changes, but no heavy-duty jib. This example belongs to a brigade workshop of 3rd Infantry Division.

The flotation screens were very vulnerable to shrapnel and other damage, particularly when erected ashore, as before the crossing of the Rhine; they also sometimes failed to collapse when required. All in all, however, they worked well, although the metal prow and screen masked the 'lap' machine gun (a Sherwood Forester can still remember a German officer who owed his life to this fact on D-Day). As units continued to fight with their DDs after landing, as normal tanks, until they were knocked out or wore out, the canvas screens were often cut away. The Staffordshire Yeomanry did this after the Rhine crossing and were subsequently somewhat embarrassed when asked to tackle the Elbe.

★   ★   ★

An 'unfrocked' DD with its flotation screens completely cut away. The metal prow has been bent down at the right front, probably to improve the field of fire of the 'lap' gun, but if so this has been largely negated by the stowage of ration boxes there.

Although these notes have been compiled from a fairly small, but not I hope unrepresentative sample of Sherman experience, it was noticeable how many of those interviewed said they had always had complete confidence in the Sherman as a tank, and how few drawbacks to it they were able to remember (a notable exception being the member of 51 RTR who had served briefly in them after a long period in Churchills). The armament and mechanical reliability were the two points almost invariably singled out for praise, and the same impression is given by many unit histories and other published work on the subject. This all tends to confirm the impression given in the wider field of campaigns in which the Sherman fought, of a tank which despite, or perhaps because of being something of a 'Jack of all trades and master of none', was arguably, overall, the most useful type to be employed by the British Army in the Second World War; and which in the long run, because of its versatility and reliability, proved a better all-round AFV than some of its more formidable opponents.

The Sherman Tank

BASIC TECHNICAL DETAILS

Length:	19ft. 4in. (average)
Width:	8ft. 7in.
Height:	9ft. 10in.
Weight:	30 tons
Max. armour:	75mm (turret) 50mm (hull)
Armament:	Basic—75mm
	'A' variants—76mm
	'B' variants—105mm
	'C' variants—17pdr.
	2 × .30 cal. and 1 × .50 cal. Browning machine guns
Engines:	Mark I & II; Wright Whirlwind radial, 400hp petrol
	Mark III; Twin GM diesels, 375hp
	Mark V; Chrysler Multibank Petrol, 445hp
Speed:	26mph
Crew:	5

Sherman V of the Coldstream Guards in early 1945 with aircraft rocket rails rigged on either side of the turret. A troop number has been roughly painted on the turret bin, and the tank tarpaulin is being used to contain and protect loose gear on the back of the hull.

The Plates

A1: Sherman II, 'B' Sqn., Staffordshire Yeomanry; El Alamein, October 1942

The Staffordshire Yeomanry were the junior regiment of 8th Armoured Brigade in 10th Armoured Division at Alamein; they thus marked in blue, following the traditional seniority sequence red, yellow, blue. (The other regiments in 8th Armoured Brigade at this time were 3 RTR and the Nottinghamshire Yeomanry.) Only 'B' Sqn. received Shermans in time for the battle, 'A' and 'C' operating Crusaders and Grants respectively. This early cast-hull M4A1, serial T74394, bears no tacsign or formation sign, according to a clear photograph; had they been carried they would have been the white '67' on a red square, and the fox's mask of 10th Armoured Division. (The two senior regiments in 8th Armoured Brigade used the tacsigns '40' and '86' at this period.) The usual 'B' Sqn. square is painted on the turret in the seniority colour; the name 'Anne' departs from normal practice in this regiment, which was to adopt names beginning with the squadron

letter, but at the time the photograph on which this picture is based was taken, this tank was in fact being used by an 'A' Squadron crew. The aerial pennants were recognition signals, and their number, colour and arrangement was specified in Operation Orders and Instructions—although tradition did play a part in the pennants flown by certain regiments. The colour scheme is Dark Green over Light Stone. This regiment was virtually wiped out during Alamein.

A2: Sherman II, 'B' Sqn., Royal Wiltshire Yeomanry; El Alamein, October 1942

Finished in overall Light Stone, this M4A1 is travelling with turret traversed to the rear. For Second Alamein 9th Armoured Brigade, consisting of 3rd The King's Own Hussars, Warwickshire Yeomanry and Royal Wiltshire Yeomanry, were removed from 10th Armoured Division and placed under the command of 2nd New Zealand

Division. They were given the task of penetrating the enemy anti-tank gun screen in the dark; as dawn broke the brigade was caught silhouetted in front of the German guns, and annihilated, but forced a vital gap nevertheless. This Sherman, T145074, is one of 13 reportedly delivered to 'B' Sqn.; its markings include the '86' square of the junior regiment in the brigade, marked on 9th Armoured Brigade's green square. The two emblems are the white horse on green of the Brigade, and the white fern leaf on black of the Division. Note air recognition roundel on engine decking; tank tarpaulin strapped along side rail; and fuel funnel attached to right rear hull. No squadron marking seems to be carried.

Troop commander's OP tank of 'C' Troop, 'Q' Bty., 55th Field Regt. RA, Guards Armoured Division, in Eindhoven. The box designed to fit on the rear hull plates of Mark V Shermans was sometimes carried at the front, as here.

B1: Sherman I, HQ 4th Armoured Brigade; Sicily 1943

For the Sicily invasion 4th Armoured Brigade was removed from 7th Armoured Division and served as an independent armoured brigade in XIII Corps; later it landed at Taranto, and fought up the Adriatic coast of Italy until December 1943, when it returned to England for pre-invasion preparation. This appears to be the Brigade Commander's tank, or that of a senior staff officer —a photograph shows the commander wearing the red-banded cap and colonel's ranking which suggest this identification. The finish is overall Bronze Green, with steel bar cleat tracks. Markings are limited to the Royal Armoured Corps red-white-red recognition flash on the nose; and above it the sign of 4th Armoured Brigade—black jerboa on white disc on black square—and the '71' on a red square of Brigade HQ. The two pennants, one low and one high on the aerial, are

red, with the central part of the Brigade sign repeated. Crew helmets and packs, and even a brown enamel mug, can be seen stowed on the front hull, strapped to the headlight guards.

B2: Sherman I, 'A' Sqn., 3rd County of London Yeomanry; Sicily, 1943

At the time of its detachment as an independent brigade, 4th Armoured Brigade consisted of the Royal Scots Greys; 3rd CLY—the 'Sharpshooters'; and 44 RTR. This colourfully-marked example is finished in Light Mud and Blue-Black. Sheet metal coamings have been welded to the edges of the rear decking to retain exterior stowage; it has the usual rounded-top stowage box added to the rear of the turret; and only the centre part of the sand shields remains intact. Serial T145884 is named 'Abdiel', and bears an individual vehicle number '6' in yellow on the turret box sides. The normal seniority colour sequence seems to have broken down somewhat, with the 'A' Sqn. triangle marked in red trimmed with yellow. Prominent RAC recognition flashes are painted on turret cheeks and hull nose. The brigade's black jerboa, facing left, is displayed high on the glacis on a white square, between the two crew positions. A single red pennant is flown at the aerial top. The tracks are of a type more usually seen on Grants, with added rubber section blocks. A length of this is attached to the hull front over the blanked-off hull aerial mounting.

C1: Sherman IIA, 'A' Sqn., 10th Royal Hussars; Italy, 1944

This rather bare-looking M3A1, with T23 turret and 76mm gun, served in the winter of 1944 with the junior regiment of 2nd Armoured Brigade, which became an independent formation in September that year when 1st Armoured Division was dispersed. The Brigade—The Queen's Bays, the 9th Lancers and the 10th Royal Hussars—fought on in Italy until the end of the war. This Sherman bears no visible markings except for the '67' on red of the junior regiment, and the squadron sign on the turret in the appropriate colour. Note the flat-topped stowage box welded to the rear of the turret, apparently supported by an iron strapping cradle fixed to the machine gun stowage arms; the lengths of piping welded on the

Even Shermans appreciated *some* maintenance! 'Cairngorm', the tank of the CO of 'C' Sqn., 116 RAC undergoes routine greasing in Burma.

hull sides, to take foliage camouflage; and the old infantry helmet worn by the commander. No pennant is flown. 'Platypus' extended grousers were sometimes fitted to every alternate trackplate in muddy areas.

C2: Sherman V of Commanding Officer, 116 Regt., Royal Armoured Corps; Burma, 1945

This regiment was raised from the Gordon Highlanders—note the tam-o'-shanter worn by the colonel in our painting. It was the senior regiment of 255th Indian Tank Brigade, serving in support of IV Corps during General Slim's victorious counter-offensive in Burma in winter 1944–45; the other regiments were Probyn's Horse, the Royal Deccan Horse and 7th Light Cavalry. The Gordons entered the campaign in February 1945, on the Irrawaddy. Tacsigns and formation markings seem to have been virtually unknown in this theatre; the CO's tank is identified only by the name on the rear hull sides, in appropriately prominent lettering. An infantry telephone is attached to the rear hull on the right, below the first aid locker; water *chagals* are slung round the turret to cool; and a large flat stowage box is fixed to the engine deck ahead of the tarpaulin.

Sherman V on the move near Meiktila with anti-mine netting rigged and Bombay Grenadier escort embarked. Burma was the only theatre where tank crews regularly wore the American-style tank crash helmet.

a–d: Formation signs

The exact shapes, colours and designs of these signs varied quite widely, as a moment's thought will make clear—they were marked on the vehicles with a huge number of different stencils or templates, over a long period of time, and as long as they were neat and recognizable few people strove for a rigid uniformity of detail.

D1: Sherman V of Commanding Officer, 1st (Armoured) Bn., Coldstream Guards; Holland, autumn 1944

The second senior regiment of 5th Guards Armoured Brigade, Guards Armoured Division in the North-West Europe campaign of 1944–45. After a certain amount of wear and tear, the difference between British 'Bronze Green' and American 'Olive Drab' became almost indistinguishable. This heavily stowed command tank has its serial, T147389, in white on the hull side above the appliqué armour which protects the ammunition stowage inside. The name 'Monck', referring to an illustrious former regimental commander, is painted rather roughly in white below the hull radio operator's hatch—note that the hull machine gun has been removed and the position

blanked over, for use by an extra radio operator in this command tank. A long aerial, striped white and khaki, is mounted on the right hull position. As was often the case, the long stowage box supplied for fitting to the rear hull has been added to the nose instead, bearing the tacsign '52' of the regiment; the HQ Sqn. diamond, in the yellow of second senior regiment in the Brigade; and the Division's formation sign. A command flag flies from one of the turret aerials. Spare track lengths are fixed vertically and horizontally around the front and sides of the turret and up the glacis plate. A thick wadding of a grey-green waste material, retained by chicken wire, is spread in untidy lengths over the hull and turret and bound round the gun. Among the front hull stowage emerging from it are a spare bogie, and, interestingly, a set of three lorry tilt-hoops strapped across the tank's nose. A final unusual feature is the sighting vane device fixed to the turret roof centrally in front of the commander's hatch. Extended end connectors are fitted to the tracks.

D2: Sherman I, '1' Sqn., 2nd (Armoured) Bn., Irish Guards; Normandy, 1944

Squadron titles in Guards regiments tended to be in line with traditional Foot Guards company practice. The junior regiment in 5th Guards Armoured Brigade, the 2nd Irish Guards named its tanks after Irish place-names beginning with A, B and C for '1', '2' and '3' Sqns. respectively. The squadron's triangle sign is marked in the blue of junior regiment, filled in black, and containing a white '2'—presumably a troop rather than a tank's individual number, as was the practice in some other Guards units. The '53' on red, the junior regiment's tacsign, is marked on the offside of the nose, and the Division's formation sign on the nearside. Between them are the name 'Ardnacrush', in white lettering, and the serial, which appears to be T147470 in the photograph we copy, but which is hard to see and much weathered. The name is repeated in the same style below the hull machine gunner's hatch. Spare track lengths are held on the glacis by retaining rods; and among the other forward stowage are a small metal box, a spare bogie, and an RAC helmet. Two aerials, striped white and khaki, are mounted on the turret. Fine mesh is wired all round the turret, and more loosely wrapped round the gun.

E1: Sherman DD, 13th/18th Royal Hussars; Normandy, 1944

On D-Day the regiments of 27th Armoured Brigade—13th/18th Royal Hussars, Staffordshire Yeomanry and East Riding Yeomanry—supported British 3rd Infantry Division in the assault on 'Sword' Beach, just west of Ouistreham. Each of the two senior regiments had two squadrons equipped with DD 'swimming tanks'. A published listing of turret numbers suggests that '43' may have been a 'B' Sqn. tank, but this is not entirely clear. It was photographed in action early in the invasion. The canvas skirts are folded down, and the propellers swung up to clear the ground; skirt supports are carried on the rear deck. Packs are slung from a turret rail and under the DD's steering platform mounted on the right rear quarter of the turret. There is a large stowage box on the rear of the turret, and a pintle-mounted .50 cal. machine gun. No markings are visible apart from the tactical number and the serial 228557DD.

E2: Sherman V, RHQ 13th/18th Royal Hussars; Normandy, 1944

Another photograph taken in the early stages of the June fighting shows us this M4A4, serial T147161, of the Hussars' regimental headquarters, which used turret numbers below '20'. 'Balaclava' was number '10'; the patch view shows how the name and a tiny HQ diamond were painted, in the red of senior regiment, above the hull appliqué armour. The 'pregnant pilchard' sign of 27th Armoured Brigade was marked on the offside rear of the hull, and the senior regiment's tacsign '51' on the nearside. Note that the lower part of the deep wading trunking is retained. The large turret bustle stowage box of this command tank has a fixed cable reel; track-plates can just be seen welded horizontally to the turret cheeks; and iron strapping cradles hold respectively a jerrycan and an oil can on the nearside and offside hull rear corners. Forward of the folded tank tarpaulin on the engine deck are a wooden crate, cardboard ration cartons and two folding wood-and-canvas beach deckchairs!

A Sherman II of 3rd CLY; the M34A1 combination gun mount and the extended end connectors on the metal chevron tracks can be clearly seen here. (Sharpshooters)

F: Sherman VC Firefly turret interior, looking forward
The huge breech and recoil shield of the 17pdr. gun filled the centre of the turret to within inches of the roof and rear, and this is omitted for clarity. See key on page 25.

G: Sherman VC Firefly driver's position; and 17pdr. ammunition stowage in right front hull position formerly occupied by machine gunner
See key on page 25.

H: Sherman VC Firefly turret interior, right and rear
Again, the 17pdr. recoil shield is omitted to allow this view; note access cut in rear turret wall for new external installation of radio set. See key on page 25.

Below: Sherman OP turret interior, left and front
A set of folding map tables were fitted in the position occupied by the main gun breech, which was removed. One of them is shown cut away here, to show the co-axial machine gun, which was retained. See key on page 25.

Notes sur les planches en couleur

Les marques des chars britanniques étaient conformes à un modèle officiel, bien qu'il y eût évidemment des exceptions à la règle. Les trois régiments dans chaque brigade avaient un ordre d'ancienneté fixe qui dépendant de leur âge respectif —c'est à dire la date à laquelle ils avaient été rassemblés. Ainsi, par exemple, *'The Queen's Bays' (2nd Dragoon Guards)*, rassemblé en 1685, était plus 'ancien' qu'un cercle pour *9th Lancers* qui n'avait été rassemblé qu'en 1715. Les escadrons au sein d'un régiment marquaient les insignes d'escadron (un triangle pour 'A', un carré pour 'B', un cercle pour 'C' et un losange pour 'HQ') en rouge, en jaune ou en bleu, selon qu'il s'agissait du premier, du second ou du troisième régiment de la brigade du point de vue d'ancienneté. Des insignes identifiaient la brigade étaient souvent peints à l'avant et à l'arrière de la coque; un numéro sur carré de couleur, normalement en blanc sur fond rouge, identifiait le régiment au sein de la brigade selon un schéma qui changeait de temps à autre. Ainsi, en Afrique en 1942, les trois régiments portaient les numéros '40', '86' et '67' par ordre d'ancienneté; en France en 1944 les numéros étaient '51', '52' et '53'. Le Sherman portait les numéros de série du fabricant américain, commençant par la lettre 'T' marquée normalement sur le côté de la coque. D'habitude, chaque char avait un nom qui lui avait été donné par son régiment; les noms commençaient souvent par la lettre A, B ou C, selon la lettre de l'escadron. Les drapeaux sur les antennes de radio étaient un moyen temporaire de reconnaissance et ils étaient souvent changés.

A1: Le régiment le moins ancien de la *8th Armoured Brigade, 10th Armoured Division*, anéanti à Alamein. Ce char ne porte aucun numéro régimentaire ni insigne divisionnaire, mais s'ils avaient été marqués ils l'auraient été comme ici—'a' et 'b'. **A2:** Le régiment le moins ancien de la *9th Armoured Brigade, 10th Armoured Division*, détaché à Alamein pour servir avec la *2nd New Zealand Division*. Numéro du régiment marqué sur carré vert; insigne de la *9th Brigade* représentant un cheval blanc; insigne de la *2nd NZ Div.*, une fougère blanche; voir la cocarde de reconnaissance aérienne sur le pontage arrière de la coque, et l'entonnoir pour faire le plein de carburant. Ce régiment également été anéanti à Alamein.

B1: La *4th Armoured Brigade* a été détachée de la *7th Armoured Division* pour l'invasion de la Sicile: ce char porte l'insigne de la brigade, représentant une gerboise noire. '71' est le numéro indicatif de l'état-major de la brigade. On croit que ceci est le char du commandant de la brigade. La barre rouge-blanc-rouge était un signe de reconnaissance britannique datant de la première guerre mondiale. **B2:** Le deuxième des régiments les plus anciens de la *4th Brigade*, mais ici le schéma de couleurs a été partiellement abandonné. Numéro de char individuel '6' et nom 'Abdiel'; triangle *A Sqn.* sur la tourelle: insigne de la *4th Brigade* marqué en haut sur l'avant de la coque. Des plaques métalliques sont soudées à chaque côté de l'arrière de la coque, pour retenir les articles rangés sur le pontage arrière.

C1: Le régiment le moins ancien de la *2nd Armoured Brigade*, ayant les marques qui ont été expliquées ci-dessus. Des sections de tuyau en fer sont soudées aux côtés de la coque, pour tenir les branches qui servaient de camouflage. **C2:** En Birmanie, les chars portaient très peu d'insignes. Le char de commandant n'est identifié que par son nom 'Coq du Nord', qui faisait allusion à l'origine écossaise du régiment: le *116 Regt. Royal Armoured Corps* avait été levé des rangs des Gordon Highlanders.

D1: Les marques sont celles qui ont été expliquées ci-dessus; le nom du char 'Monck' est celui d'un ancien commandant de régiment très célèbre; drapeau de commande régimentaire sur l'antenne de la tourelle. Le camouflage est maintenu en place par un treillis métallique. **D2:** Le régiment le moins ancien de la *5th Armoured Brigade*, l'insigne est donc peint en bleu—et '2' le numéro de peloton est dans le triangle. Le nom du char 'Ardnacrush' est celui d'un village en Irlande. Un filet en corde fine est attaché autour de la tourelle.

E1: Deux escadrons de deux régiments de la *27th Armoured Brigade*—*13th/18th Hussars* et *Staffordshire Yeomanry* furent équipés de 'chars nageants' Sherman DD pour le débarquement en Normandie le 6 juin 1944; ce char a été photographié peu de temps après, se battant en renfort de la *3rd British Infantry Division* sur la plage 'Sword'. Les 'jupes' de flottaison sont repliées et les hélices pour le voyage en mer sont rabattues pour ne pas toucher le sol. Ce régiment numérotait chaque char individuellement. **E2:** Ce char de l'état-major du régiment n'est pas un 'char nageant', mais il possède la partie inférieure d'un système d'échappement conçu pour les voyages en eau profonde. Les insignes rouges indiquent qu'il s'agit du régiment le plus ancien de la brigade; le nom du char et l'insigne d'un losange représentant le *HQ Sqn.* sont marqués en petit sur le côté; l'insigne de la *27th Brigade*, représentant un hippocampe, est à droite sur l'arrière de la coque.

F: Intérieur de la tourelle d'un Sherman VC Firefly, face à la route; la grande culasse du canon 17pdr. est omise aux fins de clarté. Voir la légende en langue anglaise qui fait allusion à toutes ces vues d'intérieur.

G: Poste du pilote d'un Sherman VC Firefly: bac à munitions aménagé dans le poste droit. Le Firefly ne portait pas de mitrailleuse et l'espace à l'intérieur de la coque qui était anciennement occupé par le tireur était utilisé de cette manière.

H: Intérieur de la tourelle d'un Sherman VC Firefly, face à l'arrière. Un trou avait été percé dans la paroi pour donner accès à la radio, qui était contenue dans une boîte fixée à l'extérieur de la tourelle, parce que le grand canon 17pdr. remplissait tout l'espace à l'intérieur. Sont également illustrés un certain nombre de tables pour la lecture des cartes géographiques qui étaient disposées à l'intérieur de la version du char Sherman adaptée à l'observateur d'artillerie, ce char ne portant pas de canon de 75 mm.

Farbtafeln

Britische Panzermarkierungen folgten einem offiziellen Muster, obgleich natürlich häufig Ausnahmen anzutreffen sind. Bei den drei Regimentern in jede Brigade gab es eine feste Rangordnung, die sich nach dem jeweiligen Regimentsalter richtete, d.h. nach dem Datum, an dem das Regiment aufgestellt worde war. So waren z.B. die 1685 aufgestellten 'The Queen's Bays' (2nd Dragoon Guards) 'rangälter' als die 9th Lancers, die erst 1715 gebildet wurden. D Kompanien innerhalb eines Regiments Kennzeichneten die Kompaniea zeichen—ein Dreieck für 'A', ein Quadrat für 'B', ein Kreis für 'C' und ein Raute für 'HQ'—mit rot, gelb oder blau, je nachdem, ob sie altersmäßig da erste, zweite oder dritte Regiment in der Rangordnung der Brigade ware Häufig wurden die Kennzeichen der Brigade oder Division auf der Vorder- un Rück-seite der Wanne aufgemalt. Eine Zahl in einem farbigen Quadrat meist in weiß und rot—kennzeichnete nach einem ständig wechselnden Cod das jeweilige Regiment innerhalb der Brigade. So trugen die drei Regimente in Afrika 1942 ihrer Rangordnung entsprechend die Zahlen '40', '86' und '67 während sie 1944 in Frankreich '51', '52' und '53' lauteten. Der Sherman tru die mit 'T' beginnende Seriennummer des amerikanischen Herstellers meiste auf der Wannenseite. Gewöhnlich gab das Regiment jedem seiner Panze einen Namen, die häufig je nachdem Buchstaben der Kompanie mit A, oder C anfing. Die Wimpel an den Antennen waren kurzzeitige Erkennung mittel und wechselten ständig.

A1: Das jüngste Regiment in der 8th Armoured Brigade, 10th Armoure Division, das bei Alamein vernichtet wurde. Dieser Panzer trägt keine Reg mentsnummer oder Divisionsabzeichen. Doch wären sie aufgemalt worden, würde sie wie hier gezeigt sein: 'a' und 'b'. **A2:** Das jüngste Regiment der 9th Armoure Brigade, 10th Armoured Division, das bei Alamein an die 2nd New Zealan Division abgestellt wurde. Die Regimentsnummer ist in ein grünes Quadra gezeichnet; außerdem ein weißes Pferd für die 9th Brigade und ein weiß Farnwedel für die 2nd NZ Div.; keine Kompanie-Embleme. Man beach das runde Lufterkennungszeichen auf dem hinteren Deck der Panzerwann und den Treibstoffstutzen. Dieses Regiment wurde ebenfalls bei Alamei aufgerieben.

B1: Die 4th Armoured Brigade wurde von der 7th Armoured Division für d Invasion Siziliens abgestellt. Dieser Tank trägt daher die schwarzen Wüste springmaus Kennzeichen der Brigade. '71' ist der Codezahl für den Brigade stab. Dies ist vermutlich der Panzer des Brigadekommandeurs. Der rot-wei rote Balken war ein britisches Panzer-Erkennungszeichen aus dem Erste Weltkrieg. **B2:** Die zweitälteste Regiment der 4th Brigade, doch wird d Farbenfolge hier teilweise nicht mehr eingehalten. Die Nummer des Panzers i '6' und sein Name 'Abdiel'; 'A' Sqn. hat Dreieck am Turm; Markierung d 4th Brigade hoch vorn am Panzerkörper. Auf jeder Seite sind am rüc wärtigen Teil des Körpers Metallplatten aufgeschweißt, die ein Herunterfalle von aug dem hinteren Deck verstauten Gegenständen verhindern sollen.

C1: Das jüngste Regiment der 2nd Armoured Brigade mit den oben erklärt Kennzeichen. Die an den Wennenseiten angeschweißten Eisenrohre dienen a Aufnahme für Tarngestrüpp. **C2:** In Burma wiesen die Panzer nur se wenige Kennzeichen auf. Dieser Kommandpanzer ist nur durch seine Namen erkennbar: 'Hahn des Nordens'—eine Anspielung auf die schottisch Herkunft des Regiments: das 116 Regt. Royal Armoured Corps wurde aus d Reihen der Gordon Highlanders aufgestellt.

D1: Kennzeichen gemäß obiger Erläuterung; Name des Panzers, 'Monck', i der Name eines ehemaligen berühmten Regimentskommandeurs; an d Turminnere auf der Regimentskommandoflagge. Die Tarnung ist mit Drahtg flecht befestigt. **D2:** Das jüngste Regiment in der 5th Guards Armoured Brigad daher Kompaniekennzeichen in Blau—hier mit Zug-Nummer '2' im Dreiec Der Name des Panzers 'Ardnacrush' ist ein irischer Dorfname. Der Turm ist m feinem Tarngeflecht umwickelt.

E1: Zwei Kompanien von zwei Regimentern der 27th Armoured Brigade—d 13th/18th Hussars und Staffordshire Yeomanry—waren für die Landung in d Normandie am 6. Juni 1944 mit 'Schwimmpanzern' Sherman DD ausgerüste Dieser Panzer wurde kurz nach der Landung photographiert. Er wurde zu Unterstützung der 3rd British Infantry Division am 'Sword'-Strand eingesetz Die Schwimmschurze aus Leinwand sind zusammengefaltet, und die Schrau ben für den Antrieb im Wasser sind hochgeklappt, damit sie nicht den Bode berühren. Die Panzer des Regimentsstabs waren die Panzer einzeln numeriert. **E2:** D Panzer des Regimentsstabs ist kein 'Amphibien-Panzer', hat aber noch d unteren Teil der Wate-Auspuffvorrichtung montiert. Die roten Abzeiche kennzeichnen das rangälteste Regiment in der Brigade; der Name des Panze und der HQ Sqn.-Raute sind klein an der Seite aufgemalt, und das Seepfer Kennzeichen der 27th Brigade, befindet sich rechts hinten an der Wanne.

F: Das Innere des Turms, Sherman VC Firefly, Blick nach vorn: der groß Verschluß der 17pdr-Geschützes ist zur Verdeutlichung weggelassen. Vg Schlüssel in englischer Sprache auf S.25, der sich auf diese Innenansichte bezieht.

G: Fahrersitz im Sherman VC Firefly, und Munitionsvorrat auf der Panzerwannenseite. Der Firefly war nicht mit einem Wannen-MG bestück und der freigewordene MG-Schützenplatz wurde auf diese Weise genutzt.

H: Turminneres des Sherman VC Firefly, Blick nach hinten. In die Panzerwan war ein Loch geschnitten, das Zugang zum Funkgerät ermöglichte, welches i einem Kasten auf der Außenseite des Turmes montiert war, denn das groß 17pdr-Geschütz füllte den Innenraum des Turmes aus. Zu sehen ist auch d Anordnung der Kartentische in der Artilleriebeobachter-Ausführung d Sherman-Panzers, der keine 75-mm-Kanone trug.